POROUS LIMESTONE BATTLEMENTS AT PYRAMID LAKE

WINTER-DRIED RABBITBRUSH IN COTTONWOOD CANYON, CALIFORNIA

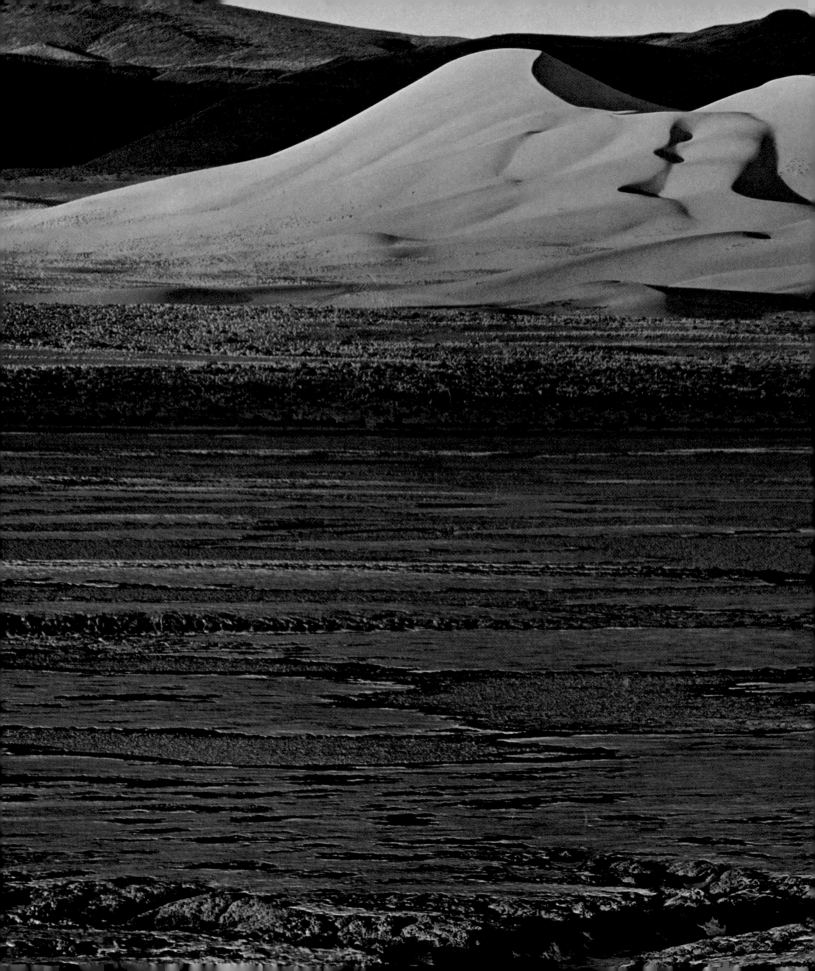

SINGING SAND MOUNTAIN SEEN ACROSS FOURMILE FLAT

DEAD COTTONWOODS ON STEENS MOUNTAIN

RIDGES CUT BY LONG-VANISHED STREAMS IN DEATH VALLEY

GOLDEN PRINCE'S PLUME AND DESERT MALLOW IN BLOOM

YUCCA AND SAGE IN RED ROCK CANYON, NEVADA

TIME
LIFE
BOOKS

SAGEBRUSH COUNTRY

THE AMERICAN WILDERNESS/TIME-LIFE BOOKS/NEW YORK

BY DONALD DALE JACKSON
AND THE EDITORS OF TIME-LIFE BOOKS

TIME-LIFE BOOKS

FOUNDER: Henry R. Luce 1898-1967

Editor-in-Chief: Hedley Donovan
Chairman of the Board: Andrew Heiskell
President: James R. Shepley
Group Vice President: Rhett Austell

Vice Chairman: Roy E. Larsen

MANAGING EDITOR: Jerry Korn
Assistant Managing Editors: Ezra Bowen,
David Maness, Martin Mann, A. B. C. Whipple
Planning Director: Oliver E. Allen
Art Director: Sheldon Cotler
Chief of Research: Beatrice T. Dobie
Director of Photography: Melvin L. Scott
Senior Text Editor: Diana Hirsh
Assistant Art Director: Arnold C. Holeywell
Assistant Chief of Research: Myra Mangan

PUBLISHER: Joan D. Manley
General Manager: John D. McSweeney
Business Manager: Nicholas J. C. Ingleton
Sales Director: Carl G. Jaeger
Promotion Director: Paul R. Stewart
Public Relations Director: Nicholas Benton

THE AMERICAN WILDERNESS
Editorial Staff for Sagebrush Country:
Editor: Robert Morton
Text Editor: Rosalind Stubenberg
Picture Editor: Patricia Hunt
Designer: Charles Mikolaycak
Staff Writers: Sally Clark, Carol Clingan,
John von Hartz
Chief Researcher: Martha T. Goolrick
Researchers: Doris Coffin, Lea G. Gordon,
Reese Hassig, Beatrice Hsia, Kumait Jawdat,
Trish Kiesewetter, Howard Lambert,
Gretchen Wessels, Suzanne Wittebort,
Editha Yango
Design Assistant: Vincent Lewis

Editorial Production
Production Editor: Douglas B. Graham
Assistant Production Editors: Gennaro C. Esposito,
Feliciano Madrid
Quality Director: Robert L. Young
Assistant Quality Director: James J. Cox
Copy Staff: Eleanore W. Karsten (chief),
Barbara Quarmby, Susan Tribich,
Florence Keith, Pearl Sverdlin
Picture Department: Dolores A. Littles,
Joan Lynch
Traffic: Carmen McLellan

Valuable assistance was given by the following
departments and individuals of Time Inc.:
Editorial Production, Norman Airey; Library,
Benjamin Lightman; Picture Collection, Doris
O'Neil; Photographic Laboratory, George
Karas; TIME-LIFE News Service, Murray J. Gart.

The Author: Donald Dale Jackson, a native Californian, traveled frequently throughout sagebrush country in the 1960s as a writer for LIFE. Born in San Francisco, he worked as a reporter for United Press International before joining the LIFE staff. In 1965 he was a Nieman Fellow. A contributor to numerous national magazines, Jackson published his first book, Judges—about the American court system—in 1974. In preparation for Sagebrush Country he made several journeys to the West, hiking and camping in Nevada and Utah.

The Cover: Dark twisted stumps of dead sagebrush interspersed with pale-leafed living sagebrush dot the foreground of Nevada's Big Smoky Valley. Farther off, the valley floor bears a coat of light brown shad scale, another of the principal plants adapted to the dry desert soil. In the far distance a midsummer thunderstorm breaks over the steep green canyons of the Toiyabe Range, one of sagebrush country's nearly 300 mountain chains.

Contents

A Vast and Varied Desert

The high, dry, 200,000-square-mile area popularly called sagebrush country but known to geographers as the Great Basin comprises nearly all of Nevada and fragments of four bordering states. Though much of sagebrush country is flat land frosted with gleaming stretches of alkali salts, the austere plains are interrupted at regular intervals by a succession of north-south mountain ranges. Some of their peaks soar over 13,000 feet, with crowns of snow that last through June and flanks that support a green blanket of grasses, juniper and aspen.

Within the borders of this diversified area lie two of the most redoubtable features of the North American landscape: Death Valley, the lowest, hottest, driest environment on the continent; and Great Salt Lake, the shallow remnant of a gigantic inland lake, whose waters are now 10 times saltier than any ocean.

On the map at left, desert areas are shown by patches of red dots. The region's lakes are color coded according to type: fresh-water lakes are white with a blue outline; salt lakes are striped and bordered in blue; intermittent lakes, which appear in times of heavy rain, are white with a broken outline; and permanently dry lake beds are stippled in blue and surrounded with a broken blue line.

1/ The Lure of a Rough Country

*Imagine a vast, waveless ocean stricken dead . . .
tufted with ash-dusted sagebushes; imagine the lifeless
silence and solitude that belong to such a place.*

MARK TWAIN/ *ROUGHING IT*

Riding across the salt flats west of Salt Lake City on his way to Nevada in 1861, a dry-mouthed Mark Twain gazed at the dusty expanse around him and thought uncharitable thoughts. He saw no beckoning forests, no dark lakes shining in sylvan hollows, no white water sculpting the boulders. What confronts the traveler over much of this land—today as in Twain's time—is space and distance and stillness, the raw reach of a primitive country filled with strange echoes. It is an arid region in which flat stretches of desert alternate with dun-colored mountain ranges; a wilderness more rugged, more stingy, more demanding than the wilderness of glade and stream.

Only one of its features pleased Twain: the silvery gray-green sagebrush that flourishes except on the highest peaks and the driest of the dry flats. Twain described the sagebrush as "an imposing monarch of the forest in exquisite miniature," a kind of live-oak tree no more than a few feet tall. And he amused himself by lying beneath one, "fancying that the gnats among its foliage were Lilliputian birds, and that the ants marching and countermarching about its base were Lilliputian flocks and herds." Though the creosote bush dominates some of the lower plains, and the ground-hugging juniper trees are common in higher elevations, it is the sagebrush that lends a special character to this land.

More than most of our surviving wilderness, sagebrush country is terra incognita to Americans, a region sadly shortchanged in our national consciousness. Its vast sprawl is part of the reason; unlike more compact wilderness areas, sagebrush country covers all of one state, Nevada, and chunks of four others: western Utah, southern Idaho, southeastern Oregon and eastern California. Despite the severity of this domain, however, within it there is diversity that can escape the eye of the casual visitor. In hidden corners of sagebrush country, snow-capped ranges abut sun-baked plains, grassy marshes adjoin parched wastes; flower-strewn canyons and alpine meadows open out onto alkali flats. Yet virtually all of it is a single physiographic province, and is so recognized by earth scientists.

In their lexicon, this entity bears the formal label of the Great Basin —a term more definitive geologically but less evocative than "sagebrush country," and indeed somewhat daunting. The Appalachians, the Mississippi and the Grand Canyon have inspired musical tributes, but no violins sing the basin's glory. It has suffered neglect in other ways as well. Though there are protected areas in the basin, no national park exists within its borders. The field guides available elsewhere are lacking here, and the map makers, too, have fallen short: parts of the basin remain imperfectly charted. Most travelers regard it as a place to get across, a charmless impediment on the route between the Rockies and California. Seldom leaving their cars, they admire the distant views, complain about the heat and press down on the accelerator.

Yet to initiates, the allure of sagebrush country is immense, a summoning of the senses so intense that it can become addictive. This was a discovery that came gradually to me as I crisscrossed the region on reporting assignments. I remember the pungent smell of the sagebrush in the early morning, the ravens playing tag in the golden glow of late afternoon, the sudden blur of a coyote digging out in pursuit of a rabbit. I recall particularly the thrill of encountering a band of wild horses grazing placidly in a hidden canyon.

Each time I returned I felt rewarded to be back, and in time I was hooked. Part of the appeal is natural—the quick splashes of color, the play of sunlight on a peak, the burst of wild flowers deep in a ravine. Part of it is something more abstract. I once worked with a Nevada native in an office building in San Francisco. Our shift was from 10 at night until six in the morning, and every night at about two he would disappear. One night I followed him and discovered his secret. He was on the roof, staring eastward past the fog-purpled neon of the city at the void beyond the lights across the bay. The stillness and sweep of the vista held him transfixed; it reminded him of home.

Sagebrush country encompasses more than 200,000 square miles. It is rimmed on the west by the Sierra Nevada, on the east by the Wasatch Mountains. The northern edge is defined by a part of the Snake River watershed; the southern edge is more elusive, but most geographers draw the line at the watershed of the Virgin River (a tributary of the Colorado) and the northernmost part of the Mojave Desert.

The area within these far-flung borders is occupied about equally by mountain ranges and broad plains, creating a colossal kind of ridge-and-valley pattern. This land form is the result of subterranean movements in this region that started some 30 to 40 million years ago, and eventually fractured the earth's crust into huge blocks. The blocks then tilted so that the lower parts eventually became plains, the upper edges mountains. This so-called block-faulting also produced breathtaking extremes of elevation. The region's highest point is 14,242-foot White Mountain Peak, near the California-Nevada line; the lowest point, only about 100 miles south, is in Death Valley, 282 feet below sea level.

The mountain ranges rise out of the dry plains at intervals of 20 to 30 miles across sagebrush country's 500-mile breadth; they are forever in view, the backdrop for every desert drama. Usually between 50 and 75 miles long and six to 15 miles wide, on a contour map of the region they look like a platoon of caterpillars scurrying southward toward the Gulf of California. Seen close up, they are considerably more impressive. The highest peaks, with tall timber and relatively abundant rain, rise to more than 10,000 feet; as a consequence, their flora and fauna have less in common with that of the basin floor than with the Rockies and the Sierra Nevada.

Below this life zone are two others, each with its own characteristic denizens. One is the zone of the high desert, which lies about 5,000 to 10,000 feet above sea level and includes both mountains and high plains; though the brown shoulders of the mountains are freckled with junipers and piñon pine, the sagebrush is undisputed master of the realm. The third zone, the low desert, lies at about 3,000 feet. A sharp demarcation line separates the desert zones. The line runs east and west about two thirds of the way down Nevada, at a point between the old bonanza towns of Goldfield and Tonopah.

While sagebrush holds sway in the high desert, in the lower country south of the Tonopah-Goldfield frontier the evergreen, yellow-flowered creosote bush takes over, often accompanied by assorted cacti and the oddly formal variety of yucca known as the Joshua tree. The boundary between the two zones is so abrupt at one point between Tonopah and

Goldfield that there is no sagebrush a few hundred feet south of it and no creosote a hundred feet north.

The high and low plains have much in common, however. Both are, in effect, smaller basins within the Great Basin; there are more than 140 of them in all. Their floors are composed of clay, silt, sand and gravel eroded from the mountains over the millennia. This process often creates broad alluvial fans on the sides of the region's ranges, graceful sloping ramps that serve as a kind of natural highway for the eroding rocks on their way down the mountainsides.

Both high and low deserts are largely treeless, except for the cottonwoods that mark the infrequent streams and springs. "Whenever a minute stream slinks for a few miles through desolation," Bernard DeVoto wrote in *The Year of Decision, 1846*, the cottonwoods' "twisting scrawl of green rises against the dead land to refresh the heart." A poetic description, but not altogether a fair one. The land does indeed appear desolate—the result of its extreme aridity—but it is far from dead. Though trees are missing, many other plants thrive, and so do certain species of animals. The secret of their survival lies in their adaptation to their harsh surroundings.

The sagebrush, for one, is a superb case study in hardihood. The dense gray hairs that cover its leaves and account for its silvery sheen impede the drying effects of the desert wind. The leaves themselves, being small, provide only a limited surface through which moisture can escape. An efficient root system is another great asset: widely radiating shallow roots quickly soak up rainfall before it can evaporate, while deeper roots draw on water sources within the earth. The creosote bush, which takes over from the sagebrush on the low desert, has its own bag of survival tricks. As the dryness becomes more intense, the bush sheds one set of soft green leaves for a second set, harder, drier and protected by a thick cuticle. If drought continues, a third set goes to work; these leaves are small, brown, and able to endure a water loss equivalent to half their weight while continuing to nourish the plant through photosynthesis.

The animals of sagebrush country, too, have adapted to the realities of its arid conditions. The most numerous are coyotes, jack rabbits, kangaroo rats and lizards. Pronghorn antelope appear on the high plains of northwest Nevada and Oregon, and the imposing desert bighorn sheep occupy the higher crags of the bare mountains in central and southern Nevada and California. These larger animals should, in theory, suffer for lack of grazing areas; instead, they nourish themselves by browsing on woody shrubs—including, of course, sagebrush.

Of the smaller animals, the coyote—cordially detested by generations of Western sheep and cattle raisers—may be the most ingenious representative of basin wildlife. Certainly it has a remarkable flair for finding whatever water the desert conceals. Sometimes the sand-laden waters of a flood runoff will collect in a pit in the desert floor and form a small pool. In time the level of the water drops, but the sand retains its contents. Somehow the coyote manages to pinpoint the place; it will then dig a hole, often a diagonal tunnel several feet deep, to get at the hidden treasure. In a sense the coyote performs a public service: many a desperately thirsty human traveler has availed himself of a coyote well, as these drinking holes are called.

Sagebrush country was not always so parched a land. There were times in its geological past, most recently from 70,000 to 100,000 years ago during the last ice age, when it had a surfeit of water. As the glaciers began to edge toward the Great Basin from the north, they were accompanied by wetter weather. The rains created many small lakes and two very large ones on the east and west sides of the basin. The eastern lake inundated nearly 20,000 square miles and covered most of what is now northwestern Utah, with extensions into Nevada and Idaho. The western lake, an estimated 8,665 square miles in extent, covered northwestern Nevada, with a finger in northeastern California.

The names conferred on these ancient lakes in the annals of geology honor two men who were, each in his own way and time, experts on the region. The western lake is called Lahontan, for Louis Armand de Lom d'Arce, Baron de Lahontan, a French aristocrat who explored the West as early as the 1680s, developed an abiding admiration for its Indian tribes, and published a book about his experiences in 1703. The eastern lake is called Bonneville, for French-born Benjamin de Bonneville, a 19th Century United States Army officer and fur trader who helped to map the Rockies.

As the last glaciers retreated, starting some 15,000 years ago, the basin's climate turned arid, and the ancient lakes began to shrink. The salt and other minerals contained in their waters—rain-washed down from the weathered mountain rocks—remain as deposits in the basin floor, creating the heavily alkaline soil that is inhospitable to all but the hardiest plants. The most visible traces of Bonneville and Lahontan —testimony to their shrinkage—are the basin's lakes. Bonneville's

A gnarled sagebrush lies dormant in the dry season, conserving water until its shallower roots can soak up the first rains.

largest remnant, Great Salt Lake in Utah, covers only 1/13 of the area of its ice-age ancestor; Lahontan's most notable descendant, Pyramid Lake in Nevada, is 168 square miles, 1/50 the size of the original.

The basin might not have remained as arid as it is except for an accident of geological history. The block-faulting that created its basic structure happened to raise the Sierra Nevada so high that they cut off the wet air moving in from the Pacific. Forced to rise, the clouds cool and dump most of their moisture in the form of rain or snow. By the time the air reaches the eastern slopes of the range, it is relatively dry. The region suffers as a result: Nevada, for example, averages only 10 to 12 inches of precipitation a year.

Unaccustomed to wetting, sagebrush country reacts to it in abrupt and sometimes violent fashion. When thunderstorms do occur, usually in summer, the runoff from a downpour can cut deep gullies in a mountainside overnight; and arroyos that are dry most of the year can suddenly roil in flood. In winter, snowmelt from the mountains will sometimes form a layer of water a few inches deep over the flatter areas called playas, which are usually dry, barren sinks of yellow-brown clay and white salt. But the thirsty soil quickly absorbs the moisture, turning the playas into treacherous mud flats. They continue to look smooth, solid and safe to cross, but the appearance is illusory. At such times roads across the playas often have to be closed. Not long ago, in northwestern Nevada, the body of one unwary driver was found on a desert road a few miles from where his car was mired in mud.

A second happenstance of geological history has profoundly affected sagebrush country, and indeed accounts for its labeling as the Great Basin. Unlike other parts of the United States, the region has virtually no outlets to the sea. Its rivers, originating in the mountain ranges within its rims, exhaust themselves in its sinks and lakes. The waters have no effective exit other than evaporation; and under the prevailing conditions of heat and dryness they evaporate in some places at the astonishing rate of 150 inches a year. This, in turn, continually adds to the abundant residues of salt in most of the region's lakes and soil; the more water that evaporates, the greater the salt concentration.

Not surprisingly, the big desert lakes have a look all their own. Most are shallow (Great Salt Lake's average depth is 13 feet), devoid of shoreline vegetation and too salty to drink. Like so much else in sagebrush country, they must be accepted on their own terms, since they defy the conventional concept of lakes as dark blue and tree bordered, with gentle waves lapping at the shore. Some of the lakes emerge so unexpectedly out of the gray-brown, treeless landscape that they seem to have materialized out of nowhere, strange desert pools that blend with the pale horizon. They don't seem to belong where they are; they appear to be some kind of cosmic afterthought.

Only one major lake in the basin meets the conventional criteria: Utah Lake, south of Salt Lake City, which looks bluer and livelier than the rest. Fed by mountain streams pouring snowmelt down from the Wasatch Range, Utah Lake also happens to have an outlet, the Jordan River. Thus, unlike Pyramid and Great Salt lakes, which have no streams flowing out of them, Utah Lake is kept constantly filled with fresh, moving water.

The region's skimpy rainfall and high rate of evaporation affect its rivers as dramatically as its lakes. Throughout most of the rest of the West, a river is a rude and muscular presence, instantly distinguishable from its milder Eastern counterparts; the Snake, for example, is to the Connecticut as a mountain lion is to a house cat. But the waterways of sagebrush country are so feebly endowed that the word river becomes an overstatement. The Truckee storms out of the Sierra as if it meant business, only to turn downright apologetic by the time it reaches Pyramid Lake. The Carson moseys along innocuously for 125 miles and then vanishes altogether in a marshy sink. And the longest of all, the Humboldt, a major guideline used in the mid-19th Century by California-bound pioneers, is so piddling that Mark Twain, who knew a few things about rivers, was moved to scorn: "A 'river' in Nevada," he wrote, "is a sickly rivulet which is just the counterpart of the Erie Canal in all respects save that the canal is twice as long and four times as deep. One of the pleasantest and most invigorating exercises one can contrive is to run and jump across the Humboldt River until he is overheated, and then drink it dry."

Sagebrush country was the last part of the contiguous United States to be explored. Its major physiographic features were first officially recorded by the explorer John C. Frémont, on two government-sponsored expeditions in 1843-1844 and 1845-1846. Of the little that was known about the region before then, some was sheer fantasy; as one connoisseur of such matters has observed, "the palpable sense of mystery in the desert air breeds fables." None other than Baron de Lahontan, in his book on the West in 1703, helped perpetuate the first of the fables. He described a large salt lake—with a river flowing out of it to the Pacific. Lahontan had seen military service in the territories of New

France, and he may have heard of Great Salt Lake from Indians; but the river he described had its headwaters in his imagination. Somehow it flowed from fiction into fact, acquired a name (the Buenaventura) and even appeared on maps, a thick line aimed resolutely west. Frémont and his scout, the legendary Kit Carson, were to spend months searching for it before concluding that it did not exist.

In the late 18th Century, two Spanish priests from Santa Fe penetrated the region as far north as Utah Lake, but the trapper and mountain man Jedediah Smith was the first to cross and recross its entire breadth in 1826 and 1827. By then the region was vaguely marked on maps as The Great Sandy Plain. Smith had no intention of exploring for the sake of exploring; what he had in mind was to seek out new sources of beaver pelts. Apparently he assumed that this would be no more difficult here than in the Rockies, which he had previously roamed as a trapper; in any event, he was ill informed about the rigors of the terrain he was entering and ill equipped to cope with them.

His subsequent report betrayed both his surprise and discomfiture. The country, he noted, was "completely barren and destitute of game. We frequently travelled without water sometimes for two days over sandy deserts, where there was no sign of vegetation and when we found water in some of the rocky hills, we most generally found some Indians who appeared the most miserable of the human race." The Indians were Paiute and Shoshone, who lived in small nomadic bands and built conical brush shelters called wickiups. Subsequent white trespassers condescendingly dubbed these Indians "Diggers," because they largely depended for their food on the roots, beetles, lizards and insect larvae they grubbed out of the ground.

Unlike the Plains Indians, the basin tribes were for the most part passive, preferring to stay out of the white man's way. Only rarely did they display any hostility, and then at some cost. In 1833 a horde of about 800 descended upon a 40-man, California-bound expedition led by the most famous of all the mountain men, Joe Walker; their objective was to avenge the killing of several tribesmen by members of the party. Walker did not condone the killings—which followed the Indians' theft of some hunting traps—but when peace parleys failed, he ordered his men to shoot. A total of 39 Indians fell in the volley of rifle fire, and the rest fled.

Except for this incident, the Walker expedition's crossing of the Great Basin was remarkably smooth—in striking contrast to Jed Smith's ven-

A tangle of tumbleweed, its bright branches contrasting with dried mud and shad-scale shrubs, bounces across Big Smoky Valley. On reaching maturity in autumn, tumbleweed plants break from their roots; as they roll before the desert wind, their seeds are jolted free to scatter on the plain.

ture six years earlier. Little more was known about the nature of the terrain by the time Walker set out, but he had a natural talent for trailblazing and was a superb planner to boot. To guard against the inevitable injury to animals along rough, rocky stretches of land, he equipped each member of his party with three extra horses as a reserve; while the expedition was still in the wooded areas east of Great Salt Lake he had the men hunt and stock up on a supply of meat—60 pounds per person.

Walker also made it a point to query local Indians he met for information about the conditions of the countryside just ahead. The route he took proved shorter than the more southerly one chosen by Jed Smith; it went across northern Nevada, following the Humboldt River and then the Carson. Many a California-bound emigrant was to benefit from Walker's trailblazing in the decades to come.

Frémont's explorations, made a dozen years after Walker under the aegis of the United States Army Corps of Topographical Engineers, gave Americans their first tantalizing insight into the region as a whole. It was, said Frémont, "surrounded by lofty mountains, contents almost unknown, but believed to be filled with rivers and lakes which have no communication with the sea, deserts and oases which have never been explored." Frémont not only deduced the peculiar nature of the region's waterways but thought up the name of Great Basin to describe it. "Interior basins with their own systems of lakes and rivers, and often sterile, are common enough in Asia," he noted with some pride of discovery, "but in America such things are new and strange, unknown and unsuspected, and discredited when related."

Frémont's reports, printed and widely circulated, were devoured by an admiring public back East; many prospective pioneers scanned them for specific guidelines to their own projected journeys. Increasingly, Frémont came to be called The Pathfinder, a nickname he delighted in. Unfortunately, his prose tended to be as flamboyant as his personality, and his facts were occasionally flawed by fables as misleading as Lahontan's story about the nonexistent Buenaventura River. The Pathfinder's description of a real river—the Humboldt—did thousands of westering pioneers a striking disservice. He pictured the Humboldt's valley as a "rich alluvion, beautifully covered with blue grass, herd grass, clover and other nutritious grasses." That sounded pretty good to an Ohio farmer who was thinking about taking his family and livestock to California, but it bore scant resemblance to the narrow desert channel the farmer found when he finally reached the Humboldt. Pioneers promptly renamed it the Humbug, and one wrote contemptuously of "scribbling asses describing nutritious grasses."

With its formidable sweep of desolation, the Great Basin was the emigrants' true testing ground. Only the crested ridges of the Sierra Nevada matched it for difficulty. The wagon trains rolled hopefully out of Missouri, followed the Platte River across Nebraska and breached the Continental Divide at South Pass, Wyoming. Emigrants bound for Oregon veered north; those bent on California turned southward and came out of the mountain trails at Great Salt Lake. The shortest route to California's verdant valleys, and its gold fields, ran right through the desert. That meant a total of 500 miles of dry basins and rugged ranges to cross before the goal could finally be reached.

The emigrants arrived at this, the harshest segment of their journey, at precisely the point when their physical strength, as well as their supplies, were most likely to be close to exhaustion. In 1846 the basin helped in the undoing of the small band of pioneers later notorious as the Donner party. They had been lured to the desert route by an enterprising California booster named Lansford W. Hastings, and the protracted and painful crossing of the dry wilderness sapped their strength and eroded their cohesion. Six weeks later they were trapped by storms in the Sierra. Of the original 87 members of the party, only 47 survived. They had turned to cannibalism to stay alive.

Many other pioneers who managed to reach California arrived destitute, their possessions yielded up to the harsh grasp of the land. The most punishing sections of those final 500 miles were the salt desert, a glaring sheen of alkali between Great Salt Lake and the eastern Nevada line, and the so-called Forty-Mile Desert of western Nevada, which began where the Humboldt disappeared into an alkali sink. At times the trail across the Forty-Mile Desert was littered with dead animals and abandoned wagons.

One 1849 pioneer, Delos Ashley, kept a diary as his party neared Humboldt Sink:

"Tues. July 17 Very warm—sand roads. Toilsome as hell.

"Wednes J 18 Sand!!! Hot!!! Grass parched & dry—

"Thurs July 19 Camped 10 P.M. No grass (wheugh!!!)

"Fri. July 20, 10 o'c Hot!!! No halt at noon. Camped 6 o'c P.M. Grass 3 ms. Spring at slough

"Sat. July 21 Staid at slough

"Sun. July 22 From slew to Sink (O barrenness)"

A few years ago, a woman I know in Nevada took part in a reenactment of the pioneers' crossing of Humboldt Sink. "I only walked a mile," she told me, "but I kept sinking to my ankles in dust. I was hot and dirty and thirsty and thoroughly miserable, but I'm sure I didn't get remotely close to how the pioneer women must have felt. There were still barrel hoops sticking out of the ground where they looked for water. I don't think I would have made it."

The basin yielded grudgingly to the white man's infiltration, but once trails had been worn and the fables dissipated, parts of the wilderness succumbed to the feverish spirit of the times. By 1848 the Mormons had built their thriving capital at the base of the Wasatch Range; in 1859 the discovery of silver created some of the West's liveliest bonanza towns; in 1860 Pony Express rider Bob Haslam raced 120 miles across central Nevada with Lincoln's inaugural address; and in 1869 the final spike in the transcontinental railroad was driven just north of Great Salt Lake. From the expeditions of Jed Smith and Joe Walker to the golden spike had taken little more than a generation.

But after another generation or so, history intervened to help the wilderness reassert itself. The attentions of men of enterprise turned elsewhere. Veins of ore played out and bonanza towns became ghost towns—the only movement in them the whirlings of *Salsola kali,* the wind-driven tumbleweed. Predictably, the only major cities in the region today—Salt Lake City, Reno, Las Vegas—hug its edges, where water and arable land are close at hand.

Allen Bruner, a tall, open-faced man in his forties, is typical of those Americans who have come to have a deep affection for the Great Basin. Bruner, a range-management researcher at the University of Nevada, lives in the low hills north of Reno, where he can occasionally hear a coyote's cry split the desert night.

In 1972 Bruner and his friend Barry Davis, a forest ranger, walked the 675-mile length of Nevada in 30 days. Publicity does not interest Bruner, and even now he finds his odyssey across the state a little difficult to talk about. "I guess I went because I love this country and its wilderness," he explains slowly, "and because I wanted to see it before anything happened to it."

Bruner and Davis had one advantage over the pioneers: they were able to plot a route that carefully skirted the Humboldt Sink. But the challenges of the journey south-to-north were demanding enough. To prepare for it, the two men went into intensive physical training for sev-

Spires of rock, sculpted by rain and ice, line the walls of Cathedral Gorge in southeastern Nevada. The spires developed after the drying up of a huge lake that once flooded the area. As the exposed rock dried, it contracted to form thin vertical crevices. Over succeeding centuries, intermittently heavy rains widened the crevices and eroded the rock surface; water trapped in the cracks froze during colder seasons and expanded them further.

eral months, gradually extending their capacity to cover long distances. The effort proved eminently worthwhile.

Every day of the hike brought fresh fascination. "You're confronted almost hourly with things you can't explain," Bruner says. "There was a dead piñon pine on a playa—why? What was it doing there? We finally figured it came down a wash in a flash flood. Another thing we puzzled about was a lot of squiggly lines in the snow with stones at the bottom of the lines. We thought about it for hours. Finally we decided that the sun's rays were melting the snow beneath the pebbles and the pebbles were sliding down, leaving a trail of lines behind them.

"We found arrowheads and old bottles. We saw coyotes, deer, wild horses, antelope, prairie falcons, golden eagles, rabbits—no cats, no rattlesnakes. Once we came upon a dead baby rabbit. I remember thinking, 'How can there be life here at all?' And here this life didn't even get started. But there's all kinds of life, you just have to look for it.

"In the south we'd walk at night, navigating by compass—just tripping through the desert. It was beautiful. The desert stillness isn't like anything else. It's complete silence—no pine needles swishing in the wind. There's a tremendous feeling of remoteness."

Partisans of the desert like Allen Bruner are rarer and less organized than partisans of mountains or forests. They are imbued with a desire to explain their appreciation of a country so often spurned as dreary and desolate. And since a taste for the desert is sublimely personal, each explanation tends to be different. My own love of the desert is inextricably bound up with the senses, with a heightened awareness of smell and color and sound (and lack of it).

The aroma of a sagebrush plain is sharp, tangy, possessed of a kind of edge that is instantly recognizable and unduplicated elsewhere. It reminded Bernard DeVoto of turpentine, but to me it suggests something indefinably sweet.

Desert colors are a symphony of light and rocks, creating and harmonizing new melodies with each passage of the sun. The rocks alone, some brought to the surface from deep within the earth's crust as a result of relatively recent igneous activity, are wonderfully varied in hue. Death Valley, for example, contains purple trachytes and volcanic tuffs that range from pure white to glowing red. Israel Russell, a 19th Century geologist who studied and itemized these rocks, once wrote some lines that reveal how the desert's colors ignite the fancy. As the sun descends, Russell observed, "every ravine and cañon becomes a fathomless abyss of purple haze, shrouding the bases of gorgeous towers and battlements that seem incrusted with a mosaic more brilliant and intricate than the work of the Venetian artists."

Night falls with astonishing sharpness in the desert. You can actually see a curtain of darkness dropping over the land—"not with a lingering twilight," Mark Twain wrote, "but with a sudden shutting down like a cellar door." And the stillness of a desert night, as Allen Bruner remarked, is duplicated nowhere else. It is so profound that it fuels irrational desires: I have felt impelled to cry out for recognition, to validate my existence.

I suppose I take a perverse satisfaction in the severity of the desert. The recognition that it demands more—more patience, more preparation, more stamina—makes it that much dearer. Self-sufficiency, the raw skills of survival, are called for here. Dealing with the desert also depends on scraps of knowledge tucked in one's brain, fused by the senses into a shimmering consciousness of place. You are aware that danger is an element, because rattlers and scorpions inhabit this region. You realize that you must *know what to do*, know where the water is and what the tracks mean.

Nothing in the desert comes easy; the Indians used to say that a man must be able to sleep in the shadow of his arrow to survive. I am always moved when I come upon a homesteader's abandoned shack, bleached and pathetic on the silent land. It seems to symbolize all the brave and poignant follies of man, the restless and foredoomed urge to conquer the unconquerable.

To savor the desert because of its harshness may be a 20th Century indulgence. Perhaps only a people who have breached the wilderness and left it behind can afford to return with fresh eyes and respect it for itself. As to why they should want to do so, perhaps Thoreau had the best answer: "It is life near the bone where it is sweetest."

Island in the Sky

PHOTOGRAPHS BY DANIEL KRAMER

To the Shoshone Indians who foraged the foothills for piñon nuts, the looming mass was known as Biatoyavi, or Big Mountain. To subsequent generations of other Nevadans, the green-mantled Toiyabe Range has been revered as "the island in the sky." It is both of those things. Rising to 6,000 feet above the surrounding desert and extending in a narrow band for 120 miles, the Toiyabes embrace a labyrinth of deep, hidden canyons and verdant stream-fed meadows that seem a world away from the baked mud and alkali of the outlying plains.

The Toiyabes' canyons, in particular, comprise a kaleidoscope of geologic forms, plants and microclimates that are an endless source of fascination to the wilderness traveler. For example, Ophir Canyon, just north of the mist-shrouded sector of the range's eastern flank shown at right, proffers a summer display of flowers to rival a suburban garden show. Only a few miles from Ophir, the bare black slate glistens like a mirror at midday, intensifying the power of the desert sun.

Within each canyon, too, different exposures create contrasting effects upon the surface of the land. South-facing canyon slopes, which receive direct sunlight during most of each day, tend to be parched and sparsely covered. But north-facing slopes, spared the full impact of direct rays, are frequently moist and green. The underlying rocks have similar effects on plant growth. The easily eroded andesite of one slope of South Twin Canyon, for instance, is more accommodating to vegetal growth than is the hard slate on the other side, where only some tenacious shrubs and grasses can take hold.

The key to the Toiyabes' many faces lies in the massif's physiography. Set on a north-south axis, the Toiyabe Range wears as its crown glacier-cut Arc Dome, which soars 11,788 feet. From the range's crest, its eastern slopes fall steeply. Moist air carried by the prevailing winds climbs the western slopes to dump as much as 25 inches of precipitation annually, nearly five times more than falls on the flats below. Over the millennia, rain, snowmelt, and ice surging down from the range's spinal crest have carved a fishbone pattern of canyons. And the rock formations they slashed into are so complex that today no two canyons are alike, either in their basic conformations or in the variety of plant life that flourishes in them.

Seen from Big Smoky Valley, the canyons hidden in the deep folds of the Toiyabes' steeper eastern flank lie shrouded in haze. The characteristic murk is caused by a combination of terpenes—natural hydrocarbon emissions from the canyons' plants —and fine dust blown up from the arid basin. It was this phenomenon that led John C. Frémont to christen the valley in the foreground Big Smoky.

In the aftermath of an early morning rainstorm, clouds disperse to reveal two small canyons (center) just below the Toiyabes' crest. Their slopes are blanketed by a patchwork of two kinds of sagebrush. The green areas are a species called big sagebrush; the pale browns are low sagebrush. The ridge dividing the canyons is mantled with the dark green of mountain mahogany; light green willow bushes line the moist canyon bottoms.

A cluster of hardy Indian paintbrush blooms on the rocky shoulder of Ophir Canyon.

Moisture-loving yellow monkey flowers spread out

Corn lilies line the edge of a sylvan nook made lush by the waters of Ophir Creek.

to follow a trickling stream midway up the canyon.

Penstemons, related to snapdragons, add a splash of color to the dry canyon walls.

Kingston Creek winds through a moist meadow in the Toiyabes. Four trout species thrive on its waters' rich nutriments: brook, brown, rainbow and a variety called Lahontan cutthroat found only in four Western states.

An orange fritillary butterfly dances on a stand of watercress blooming in Kingston Creek. Watercress floats upon the water's surface in thick mats, held together by long, intertwined roots attached to the creek's shore.

Ridges high in the Toiyabes march northeastward from Kingston Canyon, appearing alternately in sunlight and in shadows cast by passing clouds. A thin coat of sagebrush on the sunlit slopes gives them their tint.

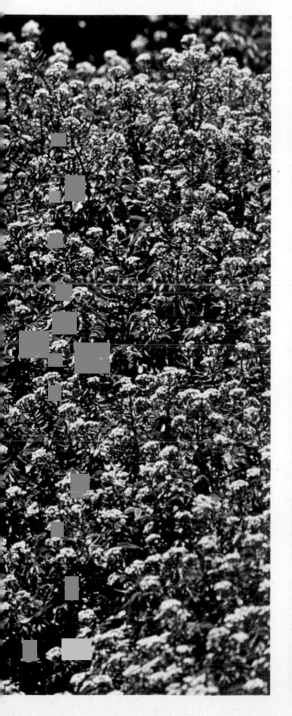

A shoulder of hard black slate rises on the south side of South Twin Canyon. The low slope on the far side of the canyon is andesite, a softer rock that rain and runoff have eroded.

On the narrow floor of its gorge, South Twin River rushes through slate beds. Minerals deposited by the flooding river have stained the slate on the right an uncharacteristic white.

Sagebrush clings tenaciously to a fractured slope of slate (left) in Jett Canyon. Weathering has split the hard rock, enlarging cracks into which runoff washes both earth and a few waterborne seeds. Only tough grasses and hardy plants like sagebrush and Mormon tea can survive here.

Twin pinnacles of quartzite tower imposingly above the entrance to McLeod Canyon (right). The ancient rock, which metamorphosed from sandstone nearly 600 million years ago, is the oldest in the Toiyabe Range.

Beyond the eastern edge of the Toiyabes, the baked, barren surface of an alkali flat glimmers in the midafternoon heat of the desert sun.

2/ A Briny Ice-Age Relic

Self-preoccupied, often sullen of mood, yet on occasion yielding itself up with an abandoned beauty that only the desert knows, it is a fit lake for a desert land.

DALE MORGAN/ *THE GREAT SALT LAKE*

It was on a day in early spring that I had my first glimpse of the Great Salt Lake. I knew little more than the obvious about it—that it is the largest lake in the United States west of the Mississippi, and incredibly salty—and I was unprepared for the changing faces it presented as I drove down Promontory Peninsula, a mountainous finger of land that juts 30 miles into the northern part of the lake.

For the first few miles my view was partially obstructed by the peninsula's hills, and all I could see of the water was a narrow band of pale blue, gleaming in the middle distance to the west. Between this band and the lake shore lay a wide zone of sulfurous-smelling gray-brown mud. Fifteen miles farther on, the mud flats gave way to the lake itself, now a blend of blue, gray and green. It was calm, eerily quiet: there were no fish breaking the surface, no birds cruising the shore. Except for occasional clumps of sagebrush and salt grass, vegetation along the shore was almost totally lacking, adding to the sense of desolation.

As I drove south, the lake changed color again, becoming greenish gray; by contrast, an irrigated meadow close to shore looked emerald. Not far from the tip of the peninsula at Promontory Point, where the road ended, the lake's color turned a beautiful Mediterranean blue. There was now a distinctly recognizable shoreline, a gravelly beach of a few hundred yards lapped by a feeble wave or two, and the vast expanse of the lake.

From the point I could see an island, a brown bulk that loomed almost straight ahead about three miles offshore. I consulted my map, was surprised to see that it showed as many as a dozen or so islands in the lake, and learned with particular pleasure that the one I was looking at was Fremont Island, where the renowned explorer had camped during his survey of the lake in 1843. I remembered reading Frémont's comment on first seeing the lake—that Balboa's men could not have been more enthralled when they sighted the Pacific—and I felt that I was sharing in the joy of discovery.

On my way back up the peninsula, at a place on the road where the water was only about 100 yards away, I yielded to a sudden impulse to test it. I got out of the car and started walking. I passed first through a line of straw-colored salt grass, then scattered sagebrush; a gray-brown chukar, a cousin of the quail that gets its name from the soft chuck-chuck sound it makes, high-stepped out of one of the bushes. Then there was more salt grass to get through, sharp bladed, tough, clearly thriving in its salty environment.

Twenty-five yards from the lake, mud took over from the grass. The mud was ankle deep, enough to slow my steps. Whenever I stopped, I could hear all around me peculiar creaking sounds, like a choir of rusty gates opening and closing. The sounds were coming from the mud. Whenever I began walking again, the noise would stop. Fifteen yards from the lake, the mud was over my boot tops. I decided to call off my projected test of the waters of Great Salt Lake and retreat. The strange, creaking chorus attended me, on and off, as I slogged back to my car.

In later weeks I tried to get from scientist friends an explanation of what I had heard, but to no avail. I suspect they credited me with an overheated imagination, and I began to wonder myself, until I found at least partial corroboration: in his book about the area, the English explorer Sir Richard Burton wrote of the "fearful submarine noises" that some of the early Canadian voyageurs reported hearing as they paddled around the lake. To this day evidently no one has solved the mystery of these noises.

In any event, my introduction to the shore of this exotic inland sea helped me appreciate some of the fascinations of Great Salt Lake: the long silent reach of it; the barrier of ooze that forbids intimacy; the dry wind, stinging with salt; the swiftly changing colors, varying with season and time of day, with cloud formations and atmospheric conditions, with the differing species of algal life in the waters. And the lake has contradictory moods: it can be sparkling or sluggish, inviting or surly, serene or stormy. It is a place as difficult to know as the desert it lies in, and as meager in its rewards.

The lake's most celebrated quality is, of course, its salinity. The only landlocked body of water in the world with a higher salt content—and it is only slightly higher—is the Dead Sea. The salt in Great Salt Lake comes partly from the old salt beds of its ancient predecessor, Lake Bonneville, and partly from the rocks that line its feeder streams. Most rocks contain minute amounts of salt, produced by the chemical weathering of the minerals in the rocks. In this case rain and melting snow in the nearby Wasatch Range and other mountains transport the salt, in solution, to the rivers that flow out of the mountains and into the lake.

The sheer size of the lake—about 50 miles wide by 75 miles long—makes it an immense reservoir for the incoming waters and their salt cargo. But then the waters have no place to go. The lake's lack of an outlet means that their only escape is by evaporation. The salt remains. Astonishing as it may seem, all the salt accumulated in and around the lake through the millennia is still there, and more is accumulating. The present quantity is estimated at eight billion tons, either in the lake, under it or on its fringes. A related and no less remarkable statistic: the lake has an average salt content of about 25 per cent, roughly one part salt for every three parts water, compared with a ratio for the ocean of one part salt to 30 parts water.

Swimmers in Great Salt Lake are pleased to find themselves unable to sink—a phenomenon caused by the salt-saturated water—but they complain when the brine burns their eyes and throat and the salt clings to their skin. In the 19th Century the dauntless Richard Burton, who ducked below the surface with both eyes open, was obliged to report: "At first there was a sneaking twinge, then a bold succession of twinges, and lastly a steady, honest burning."

Sailors as well as swimmers can have their problems on the lake. It is so shallow—only 32 feet at its deepest point, less than half that in most places—that voyages across its waters are restricted to shallow-draft vessels, and the salt can put an outboard engine out of action quickly. Still, boats have traveled the lake for over a century: the inflatable rubber dinghies and buffalo-skin "bull boats" of the early explorers were followed by freighters, ore steamers and pleasure craft. Boating and swimming alike have depended in part on the whim of storms—which occur year round, often arising with sudden ferocity and kicking up waves as high as eight feet—and in part on the changing water level of the lake. In fact, some resorts that were built along the south shore and enjoyed considerable prosperity around the turn of the century had to be abandoned as the water receded in the 1930s and again in the 1960s.

The drying trend that eventually put the resorts out of business dates from as far back as the late 1870s. Its persistence has given rise to glum forebodings that at some point in the dim future the lake may dwindle to a mud puddle, then turn into a playa like the adjoining desert. Some scientists who have been predicting the lake's eventual demise cite not only the long-range drying trend but also the effect of irrigation projects that divert its feeder streams. The reasoning seems entirely sound, but the lake continues to confound the prophets. Over the years its water level has constantly fluctuated—some years falling, but other years bobbing up again.

A closed-basin lake finds its water level through a balance of evaporation and precipitation. Since Great Salt Lake's evaporation rate is a fairly constant 40 inches a year, its level is determined by the varying amounts of precipitation it gets. In 1850, when annual statistics began to be compiled, the surface of the lake lay at 4,201 feet above sea level. In the years since, the elevation graph has shown dips and rises in a totally unpredictable sequence. In 1873 the lake lay at nearly 4,212 feet, highest in its recorded history. It was down to 4,197 feet in 1905, back up to 4,205 feet in 1924, and back down to 4,194 feet in 1940. In 1963 it lay at 4,192 feet, the lowest in its recorded history. Yet in 1973 the lake rose up again to 4,201 feet—precisely where it had been in the year that the record keeping began.

Such variations profoundly affect the size of the lake; one mathematical wizard has figured that a 10-foot change in the water level, up or down, adds or subtracts 240 square miles of lake area. As more of the lake bed is covered—or laid bare—the shoreline changes accordingly in look and location. The islands in the lake, too, undergo alteration; when the water is low, some of them turn into extensions of the mainland. The second largest—Stansbury, which spreads over more than 22,000 acres—has been masquerading under false pretenses for decades. It is no longer an island but a peninsula.

Man as well as nature has been responsible for changing the look of Great Salt Lake. In 1903 it was split into northern and southern segments by the 102-mile Lucin Cutoff, so called after a town west of the lake. The cutoff was just what the word implies: a means of shaving mileage off the transcontinental railroad route—44 miles, as it turned

Seen through the low-lying brush on the beach of Antelope Island, the peaks of Stansbury Island stretch across the Great Salt Lake horizon. The two islands, only 14 miles apart at the farthest reach, vary markedly in climate. Westerly winds, which bring six inches of annual precipitation to Stansbury, pick up additional moisture as they continue eastward across the lake, depositing two and a half times more rain and snow on Antelope.

out. The route not only was shorter, but also avoided the heavy grades in the mountainous terrain to the north.

A lot of labor and materials went into the building of the cutoff: a force of 3,000 men, timber from 38,000 trees and hundreds of trainloads of rock. From time to time the lake exacts its revenge for this incursion on its quietude. Its waters are so dense that when they are churned into waves by a storm, their impact is powerful enough to move the massive boulders beneath the roadway, keeping repair crews busy throughout the year.

Both the level of the lake and its salinity determine the forms of life that can exist in its waters. The most rudimentary are algae and bacteria, which are partly responsible for producing the lake's phenomenal color variations. One variety of algae is pink, another a near turquoise. On occasion large parts of the lake are the color of rosé wine—courtesy of some bacteria of that hue.

A rung or two higher on the lake's ladder of species are the brine flies, known locally as buffalo gnats. Their decomposing larvae line the shore in appallingly abundant heaps, emitting a rancid odor that makes a lasting impression on anyone who encounters it. One of the first to take offense was Army Captain Howard Stansbury, who made a survey of the area in 1849 and reported bleakly that "the whole air is poisoned" with the fetid stench. The problem persists to this day, and there is much talk of ridding the lake of these offensive insects. But no one has figured out a way to do so without seriously disrupting the lake's food chain.

Tiny pink shrimp, no more than a quarter inch long, constitute a less vexing segment of the lake's population. They swarm below the surface in such masses that they resemble underwater ledges of pink rock. "You can dip a cup in the lake in the summer and come up with a hundred of them," a Great Salt Lake sailor told me. Their eggs are sold to hatch as tropical-fish food, but the shrimp themselves have as yet managed to avoid ending up in cocktail sauce: they are too small and too salty. One 19th Century gourmet cooked them in butter and pepper and pronounced them "actually delicious," but he appears to have been in a discriminating minority.

No fish whatever live in the briny broth of Great Salt Lake. A fish must maintain a balance between the salinity in its system and that in its environment, and in the present salt concentration of the lake its cells would shrivel. Fish occasionally wander into the lake from a feed-

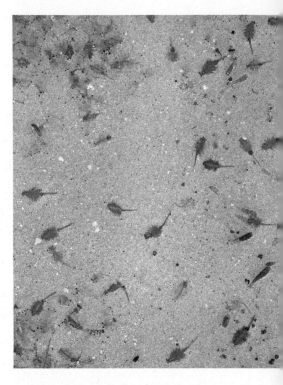

Quarter-inch-long brine shrimp, looking like bacteria on a microscope slide, lie stranded and dead on the sandy shore of Great Salt Lake, where wave action has left them high and dry. Extending from their tiny bodies are hairlike appendages that the shrimp use for propulsion, breathing, and straining algae and other food from the lake's excessively briny water.

cr stream, but they die quickly; their skeletons sometimes wash up on the shore. Undeterred by such futile sights, Utah residents have made energetic attempts to stock the lake with everything from oysters to eels. The waters of the "briny shallow," as one early Mormon called the lake, have killed them all.

The real wildlife action at Great Salt Lake is in the air. With the onset of spring, white pelicans by the thousands fly in to breed on Gunnison Island, in the northwestern part of the lake. Somewhat isolated from the rest of the lake by the Lucin Cutoff, Gunnison offers the birds security from predators and barren stretches in which to land and take off. At least three of the lake's other islands serve as rookeries, accommodating the nesting needs of hordes of blue herons, cormorants, Caspian terns and California gulls.

The gulls, taken for granted along the seaboard, have a special place in the hearts of Utah residents, and are in fact protected by state law. The reason for their esteem stems from the time a flock of them swooped in from the west and gobbled up the crickets that plagued the crops of the first Mormon farmers—a feat that has earned the gulls local celebration as "the Mormon Air Force." Curiously, they are one of the few species of birds that derive some nourishment from the flies and shrimp in the lake. Most other incomers reject this kind of diet and must satisfy their appetites by poking around in the fresh-water streams and marshes on the lake's fringes.

One of their most reliable larders is at Bear River Migratory Bird Refuge, a sanctuary maintained by the U.S. Fish and Wildlife Service at the northeastern end of the lake. The refuge, which was set up in 1928 as a way-stop for ducks and dozens of other migratory species en route to such scattered precincts as Siberia, South America and the eastern United States, covers some 65,000 acres. Its shallow ponds abound in carp and catfish, a boon not only to the migrants in residence but also to the bird colonists on the lake islands.

I watched a pelican glide low over the ponds at the refuge, its body stretched in a long, smooth line, its neck curved gracefully. Unlike its relative the brown pelican, which dives from the air when it spots its prey in the water, the white pelican first lands, then swims about in search of a morsel. The pelican I saw was even more deliberate in its movements; every now and then it would stop and scan a likely area for fishing. The strategy worked well: when last I saw the bird, it was gliding off with several fair-sized carp in its ample bill. As I turned to go, I discovered that I was only one of several interested onlookers. A bald eagle stood motionless but alert on a muskrat mound, while at a respectful distance from this formidable monarch of the air some Canada geese fluttered and chattered.

A durable mountain man named Jim Bridger is credited with being the first white man to see the Great Salt Lake, and he was there only to settle a bet. In 1824 Bridger was with a party of trappers on the Bear River in southern Idaho, about eight miles northeast of the lake, when an argument developed about the river's course. One group maintained that it emptied into the ocean; the other claimed that its outlet was an inland lake. The contenders backed their opinions with cash, and Bridger was delegated to follow the river to its mouth. He reached the lake at what is now called Bear River Bay, on the northeast arm, took a drink of the salt water, quickly spat it out and returned to his friends to report confidently that the Bear emptied into the Pacific.

Bridger's conclusion survived until another band of trappers circumnavigated the lake two years later, scouting for beaver streams. They found several streams flowing into the lake but none flowing out. Despite this finding, the belief persisted that there was a link between Great Salt Lake and the Pacific—that a terrible whirlpool in midlake led to an underground channel to the ocean.

That was only one of many legends that lingered. Even to the local Gosiute Indians, who knew the lake better than anyone else, it was a place of vague but palpable menace. They called it Pia-pa (Great Water) or Titsa-pa (Bad Water), depending, no doubt, on their most recent experience with it. The early white explorers fostered a number of stories about it. Giant Indians mounted on elephants, as well as a tribe of white Indians called the Munchies, were said to reside on its islands. There were tales of unearthly storms whipping its surface and of huge drains on the bottom, like plugs in a bathtub, through which the lake's waters periodically disappeared.

Even the usually self-confident John Frémont cranked up a considerable head of apprehension before he first beheld the lake. Stories fed to Frémont by the mountain men who served as guides on his 1843 expedition had been campfire conversation for weeks, and he wrote in his journal that "my own mind had become tolerably well filled with their indefinite pictures, and insensibly colored with their romantic descriptions, which, in the pleasure of excitement, I was well disposed to believe, and half expected to realize."

When Frémont actually came upon the lake from the northeast in

White pelicans nest between tufts of salt grass in March after arriving at their summer rookery on Gunnison Island in Great Salt Lake.

Cedar on the south; Lakeside and Hogup to the west; Promontory and Hansel on the north. Some of the lake's ancient history is notched on their walls in the form of wide gravel terraces; at one time or another in the dim past these were the beaches and shoreline of Lake Bonneville, Great Salt Lake's ice-age antecedent. There are about 50 of these terraces; the highest, known as Bonneville Terrace, lies 1,000 feet above the present lake's surface.

My own choice of a vantage point from which to take a long look at the lake was the Lakeside Range. The highest peak in the Lakesides rises to 6,625 feet above sea level, more than 2,400 feet above the lake. The mountains slope down to the lake from the southwest, separated from the water by the inevitable mud and salt flats. They are typical desert mountains. Springs are almost nonexistent. The soil of the slopes and canyons is dry, rocky, sandy, and it harbors only such vegetation as can endure these conditions: sagebrush, of course, and mountain mahogany and juniper trees. Junipers in other parts of the United States may grow as tall as 50 to 100 feet. The desert juniper—also called the Utah juniper—seldom exceeds 15 feet and more often grows only six to 12 feet, with stiff, low-lying branches and ashy gray bark.

I could not have found a more expert guide for my trip to the Lakesides than John Carlson. He is by training a botanist and by inclination an uphill racer—a hiker of great determination and energy. His job as area manager for the Federal Bureau of Land Management's Salt Lake district affords him a certain liberty to tramp the dry hills and deserts around Great Salt Lake while getting paid for it—a fringe benefit that keeps him contented. He is incorrigibly sunny-natured, a man given to sudden whoops of unrestrained joy when detached from civilization.

We parked our Jeep at the base of a canyon and started up the side, picking our way through thickly packed juniper. I looked back at the lake. Clouds of varying degrees of menace rolled over it, but the waters themselves appeared calm, tinted a soft gray-blue like a Japanese print. The Mormon Air Force was conducting maneuvers over the mud flats.

Carlson's customary uphill gallop slowed intermittently as he paused to point out different plants, all hardy species: black sage, bluebunch wheat grass, Indian rice grass and rabbitbrush. "This is called climax vegetation," he explained. "It's a closed community from the standpoint of water. The bare places between plants show that there isn't enough water for anything else to grow."

"If animals overgrazed this area," he continued, "they would elim-

A thin, sun-baked crust atop the five-foot-deep layer of salt on Bonneville Flats crinkles into ridges that rise up to a foot in height.

A terrace partway up a hillside at the south end of Salt Lake Valley marks the wave-carved level once reached by Lake Bonneville.

inate the wheat grass and black sage. That would create an opening, and plants the animals don't favor, like juniper, would increase." He frowned. "Then the invaders would arrive, snakeweed maybe or prickly pear, plants the animals won't eat."

A light rain began to fall as we climbed farther up the canyon. A party of slate-colored juncos twittered and squeaked along the limestone canyon wall. At one point I glanced back at the lake and saw to my surprise that it was smooth as glass, and reflected no clouds. The clouds were with us instead.

We reached a ridge and paused. Uphill Racer was happy. "It pleases me just to be here," he declared. "You can see a hundred miles from this spot." Below us, to the east, lay the lake; to the west lay the flats of Great Salt Lake Desert. A long freight train moved silently across it; no other signs of man were visible. The bare gray-white skin of the desert, some parts glistening in sunlight, other parts in shadow, stretched to the horizon and beyond, reaching into Nevada.

We were on an ecological island between lake and desert; in fact, the peaks we were climbing were once islands in Lake Bonneville. Carlson pointed out the terrace lines of the ancient lake. "It's unreal, that damn lake," he said. "Just imagine how big and deep it was."

He fell silent, then spotted something at his feet. He bent down and picked up a piece of desiccated coyote scat, which he carefully dissected. "Look at that," he said. "It's all hair. Poor devil must have been hungry." He scanned the vista below us. "This old boy comes up here and just sits and watches, looking for rabbits, deer, anything. It's his campsite. He's probably watching us now."

We began to climb again, and after a while reached another ridge. We were close to 6,000 feet now, and there was a light dusting of snow on the rocks. We traversed a saddle from which we were able to get a second, higher view of the lake on one side and the desert on the other. Carlson pointed to an innocuous-looking plant with three long leaves. "Death camas," he said. "It belongs to the lily family, but it's deadly poison to grazing sheep."

Wind blew through a juniper grove below us, and I glanced at the sky. Two squall clouds rushed over the lake, dipping toward the water like tornado funnels. The lake now looked a pale greenish blue. "I've seen it the most brilliant, gorgeous blue you can imagine," Carlson said, "and other times pure turquoise. I've sailed on it and swum in it. If you swallow that water you feel as though you're strangling. You feel as though you can't clear the salt out of your mouth. Perhaps it's some sort of mental block."

We headed uphill again, reaching a pass, still snow-carpeted in April, that was lined with limestone boulders on its edges, like the protective rim of a fortress. Cliff rose, an evergreen shrub with delicate flowers of a creamy color, poked through the snow. Uphill Racer, forever curious about what lies around the next bend, was maintaining a brisk pace. I saw him stop and study the snow. "Mule-deer tracks," he said as I came up. "They must use this as a crossing."

We were within a few hundred feet of the highest point in sight. A ferruginous hawk warily circled an outcropping of rimrock ahead of us, emitting sporadic squawks. "That must be where the nest is," Carlson said. "Those are distress cries—it's bothered by our being here." The hawk floated lazily in the breeze, keeping us in view. Hawks will usually attack to protect their nests, Carlson explained, while eagles will more readily abandon a nest if disturbed. The hawk passed between us and the emerging sun, casting a shadow on the snow, then glided back to the rimrock.

We plodded on, searching for a campsite on the lake side of the peak. Uphill Racer gathered up some bright green stems from a low bush. "Mormon tea," he said. "We'll have some tonight." The rain had stopped and the late-afternoon sun was deepening the colors of the rocks to rust and chocolate brown.

At length we found a relatively level ledge just below the jagged peak, dropped our packs and built a fire with juniper branches. We boiled a pot of water and soaked the Mormon tea in it. It tasted like a grassy bouillon mildly spiced with onion.

The peak of our own mountain was just behind us, but to the front and sides our view was unobstructed. We counted four separate mountain ranges: the Wasatch, dark and powerful, filling the eastern horizon; and to the southeast and south, the Oquirrh, the Stansbury and the Cedar. A new brigade of clouds was moving over the lake, bumping and jostling each other in the pale sky. "The only thing that tarnishes this view is that lead mill," Carlson said, indicating a squat building near the lake's west shore. Dark smoke rose from its chimneys. Carlson smiled and pointed. "But look how that big old cloud dwarfs the factory. Man, if it just sat down on that son of a gun it'd smother it."

The sky was streaked with black in the sunset glow. Lights blinked on in the cities along the base of the Wasatch—Bountiful and Farmington and Ogden—a few miles east of the lake. The stillness was absolute. In the fire glow a narrow column of rimrock behind us looked like a totem pole; the play of light on its pitted surface gave it momentary facial features. We pitched our tent between a juniper tree and a limestone cliff.

In the morning we arose to see great puddles of light advancing westward across the lake. The sky was clear. I saw now that dead juniper branches littered the slope below us like driftwood. A chorus of juncos saluted the day.

"I have a special concoction I usually brew up for breakfast," Carlson announced. "I use three raw eggs, twelve ounces of milk, a banana and protein supplement. Mix it all up in a mixer. But I left it home." I managed to suppress my disappointment at this news and turned to collecting my gear for the trip back.

A few minutes later I heard the sound of fervent song coming from a point several yards up the side of the cliff. "O ye mountains high, where the clear blue sky arches o'er the vale of the free. . . ." I glanced up and saw Uphill Racer beaming. "It's a Mormon song," he explained. From our respective vantage points we gazed out at the lake. It was pale blue again, and perfectly serene.

I remembered something I had read years before, the words of naturalist Joseph Wood Krutch describing desert country and what ecologists might call "an unfavorable environment." Krutch mused: "Unfavorable for what and for whom? For many plants, for many animals and for some men it is very favorable indeed."

For Carlson, and for other men like Lambourne in his solitude on Gunnison Island, Great Salt Lake has been very favorable indeed.

Assault on a Stubborn Wilderness

To the men and women who pushed west during the 19th Century, the forbidding stretch of ground between Utah's Wasatch Range and the Sierra Nevada was not known by its wilderness designation of sagebrush country. Rather it was regarded, with no particular love, as the trackless expanse called the Great Sandy Plain. Yet for all its hot, cold, waterless, dust-blown façade, this apparently inhospitable country acted as a powerful magnet for a wide range of willing adventurers.

There were the emigrants, most of them bound for California. As they crossed the parched wastes of the Forty-Mile Desert, their oxen dropped in their yokes from the heat and the strain of pulling the heavy wagons, and men were blinded by the fine alkali dust that never seemed to settle from the air. Some of the emigrants, particularly Mormons (right), took to the harsh country, irrigated its arid soil and established the flourishing city of Salt Lake.

Then there were the miners, who rushed into jerry-built camps like Virginia City, Nevada, to tear silver from the earth (page 74). Like a score of other mine towns in sagebrush country, Virginia City boomed for about two decades, and then precipitously declined: its population, rising to about 25,000 in 1876, now stands at nearer 500.

There were the explorers and surveyors such as Clarence King (overleaf), who set out along the 40th parallel in 1867 as head of a United States government expedition to map a 100-mile-wide swath of this territory. And there were the railroad men, ruthless empire builders whose passion was to conquer the wilderness, forge a commercial link between the coasts—and make plenty of money along the way.

Perhaps most intriguing of all was the small band of 19th Century photographers, pioneers in their own right—men like Timothy O'Sullivan, who accompanied Clarence King and took the pictures on pages 72-73. Their mission was to take nothing from the wilderness beyond a record of its grandeur. And this they did, carting their crude but effective equipment into the raw terrain. More celebrated adventurers left behind far less of value than did these earliest recorders of the appearance of sagebrush country.

A Mormon wagon train descends from the Wasatch Mountains toward Salt Lake City. By 1867, when this picture was taken, the Mormons had settled down in the area, but others continued west. Emigrant wagons needed about five weeks to cross sagebrush country. En route they faced heat, thirst, fatigue, Indians, malaria, cholera and an endless swirl of alkali dust.

The vast sweep of Nevada's Dixie
Valley dwarfs the outsized camera (far
left) and the wagon darkroom of
Timothy O'Sullivan, photographer for
a United States government survey
team during the late 1860s. Despite the
heat and the dust, the survey's young
leader, Clarence King (above)—a
recent Yale graduate—often insisted on
dressing for dinner in proper Eastern
gentleman's attire, complete with
derby, whenever guests were present.

At the entrance to a shaft in Virginia City, Nevada, a miner examines a vein, perhaps of the silver that formed the fabled Comstock Lode. At the mines' peak in 1877, the silver ore was so rich that workers sometimes stole $1,000 worth a day by stuffing it into their pockets, but within three years the mine's heyday was over.

It was in the 1880s that 20-mule teams began to haul borax over the 165 miles of hills and desert from Death Valley to a railhead at Mojave, California. Their 36-ton loads for the 10-day trip included 1,200 gallons of water to keep the draft animals from collapsing of dehydration: midday temperatures often reached 120° F.

A track-laying crew for the Central
Pacific Railroad (above) speeds
its work. The Central and Union Pacific
crews had their historic meeting
at Promontory Summit, Utah (right),
where the first transcontinental
railway was completed on May 10, 1869.
Though the event was hailed as
a key step in the subjugation of
the wilderness, sagebrush country has
never surrendered. The site of this
meeting has long since fallen into
disuse, the right of way reclaimed by
jack rabbits and tumbleweed.

3/ Jewel in the Desert

Mountains are seen beyond, rising in bewildering abundance, range beyond range . . . and nowhere may you meet with more varied and delightful surprises than in the byways and recesses of this sublime wilderness.　　　JOHN MUIR/ *STEEP TRAILS*

The Ruby Mountains burst out of the barrens of eastern Nevada in a joyous eruption of green and white, gaudy strangers on the dun-brown landscape. With their steep-walled peaks, banded by snow for as much as 10 months of the year, and their flanks thick in forest, they seem like an errant spur of the Rockies that has strayed into sagebrush country. They are everything that the adjoining desert is not: lush, snow washed, lake spangled, as welcome a sight as an old friend in a strange town.

The Rubies' resemblance to classic mountain wilderness is primarily due to the unusually heavy precipitation their high peaks receive—up to 35 inches a year, compared to the 10-inch annual average for the state of Nevada itself. They are not the only peaks in the Great Basin to be so favored. The Snake Mountains to the east, for example, get 45 inches a year, the Toiyabes in central Nevada 25 inches, and both ranges are accordingly verdant. But for me there is a special appeal in the Rubies, in the vivid contrast between their moist, bountiful massif and the dry desert plains that border the range. It was this beguiling juxtaposition that first lured me to the Rubies.

I had a more specific mission in mind as well: I hoped to track down a bristlecone pine, the oldest-known living species of tree—of anything, for that matter—on earth. I knew that bristlecones are found in the Rockies and elsewhere in the West, but I had been told that the Great Basin variety is far and away the longest lasting, so much so that it has been designated a separate species—*Pinus longaeva*. Some time ago, on Wheeler Peak in the Snake Range, a bristlecone estimated to be 4,844 years old was inadvertently felled. Another venerable specimen, aged 4,600 years, was said to be still clinging to a strand of life in the White Mountains near the California-Nevada line. In my earlier wanderings through sagebrush country, the bristlecone had totally eluded me and I was beginning to feel that I might never see one.

Then Alvin McLane, with whom I planned to travel the Rubies, mentioned the likelihood of seeing an example or two of this Methuselah of the pine family there. Alvin, I thought jubilantly, should know. He had worked as a hydrologic-geologic assistant at the Desert Research Institute of the University of Nevada in Reno. Much of his time was spent charting the mountains in the state, some of which are still not to be found on maps. Though he was born an Easterner, he has lived in Nevada since 1958, and he is probably more familiar with its wilderness areas than are most native sons.

Certainly, when I met him for a briefing session before we set out, he had all the basic facts about the Rubies right at his fingertips, beginning with the reason for their name. A company of United States Army soldiers, camping in the mountains in the 1840s, decided to do a bit of prospecting in their off-duty hours and came upon some shiny, deep red minerals that they identified as rubies. This might have touched off the kind of bonanza that swept other ranges in sagebrush country—except that, in the course of a more expert examination, the rubies proved to be garnets. By then, however, the Rubies had their name and, fortunately for the romantics among us, it has stuck.

Garnets, beryl crystals and other gem stones still turn up today, Alvin told me, but he personally finds a lot more interest in the plain old rocks that make up the mountains. I must have looked slightly skeptical, as nongeologists tend to do at such remarks. However, as I was to learn over the next several days, my friend McLane always has a ready explanation. "For one thing," he said, "some of the rocks are Precambrian." He paused somewhat dramatically. "Very old?" I asked. "Very," he said. "Formed about a billion and a half years ago." I was impressed; suddenly the 4,000-year-or-so-old bristlecone pine I was hoping to spot in the Rubies seemed a mere babe. Alvin pursued his point. There are only a few ranges in sagebrush country where Precambrian rocks are exposed at all, he informed me, and in the Rubies they are more extensively exposed than anywhere else in the whole region.

Another distinction of the rocks in the Rubies is the way they are distributed. The range is 90 miles long, with northern and southern sections, divided about two-thirds down the length by a lofty corridor called Harrison Pass. During the mountain-building period that raised up the Rubies about 30 to 40 million years ago, the rocks that went into their making were aligned in a pronounced north-south pattern. South of Harrison Pass, the mountains are partly sedimentary shale and sandstone, but mostly limestone, laid down in ancient seas that covered the area from time to time. North of the pass, the rocks are harder: granite and such metamorphic types as gneiss and schist and quartzite, their original texture and composition changed under the intense heat and pressure of mountain-building processes.

Having given me this short and simplified lesson in the geologic past, Alvin now proceeded to explain its bearing on the present. "Because the rocks are different," he said, "the northern and southern arms of the Rubies are different. It's much greener and wetter in the northern section because the surface water isn't absorbed by the hard rock there as it is by the limestone in the south. There's a great deal more runoff and more accumulation."

Most of the 29 lakes and ponds in the range are north of Harrison Pass, and the abundance of water supports more flowers, more birds and more animals than in the south. Clearly, the north was Alvin's preferred choice for my introduction to the Rubies.

We reached the heart of the northern Rubies by way of Lamoille Canyon, a glacier-sculpted valley on the relatively gentle western slope of the range. As I took in my first view, I found it hard to believe. The canyon walls were a closely woven tapestry of dark and light green—dense stands of mountain mahogany interspersed with paler aspen trees. On either side, dozens of little waterfalls spilled down the creased and layered rock above the trees. Though I had expected contrast, I had not reckoned on so swift a change of scene as this. Only a short while before, our Jeep had been traveling through treeless, shadeless desert; dust and the scorching heat of a summer morning had dogged us almost all the way up the winding road to this green haven.

"Thousands of people shoot by on the highway through Elko and don't even know that this canyon is only 20 miles away," Alvin said. He gazed up at the forested, half-moon-shaped cirque at the head of the canyon. The steep walls there had once marked the upper terminus of the glacier that had gouged out this valley. Now, though the month was July, broad snowfields clung to the heights of the walls and dark clouds

Dusted by early snow, a rocky ridge of the Ruby Mountains is mirrored in one of several round alpine ponds known as the Dollar Lakes.

nudged the peaks that loomed beyond. "It can snow any day of the year in here," Alvin said.

We parked the Jeep where the road ended near the base of the cirque. A U.S. Forest Service sign informed us that the elevation here was 8,850 feet, which meant that we had already come up about 3,000 feet from the high plain bordering the mountains. We unloaded our gear, stowed it in our backpacks, and set out on a trail leading to the top of the canyon and into the mountain meadows beyond. Almost at once we had to cross a swift-flowing stream, its banks brightly lined with bluebells and yellow-flowered senecio. I thought again of the parched desert we had left behind. Alvin was smiling.

A soft rain started to fall. As we climbed, the mountain mahogany and the aspen gradually disappeared and a small tree with a low, bushy trunk began to dominate the landscape. "We've moved out of the life zone of the mahogany and aspen," McLane explained. "Their upper limit is about 8,800 feet. We're in the subalpine zone now. This tree you see everywhere is a kind of white pine."

At the mention of pine, I looked around hopefully and Alvin read my mind. "No, not bristlecone," he said, "limber pine." He bent a slim, low-hanging branch from one of the trees along the trail and tied it into an overhand knot. "See why they're called limber. You can tie a limb in a knot and it won't snap."

Our trail had become a series of switchbacks through pine groves and along rock ledges, and here and there small snowbanks lay athwart our path, with rivulets seeping from them—the first links in the water chain that ultimately forms the Humboldt River, 24 miles to the north. The snowbanks were easy enough to hurdle, but the more extensive snowfields that spread higher up were more formidable. We were able to detour around two of them, but then had to mush across a 100-yard-wide band of snow on a bare slope, angling perhaps 5° upward. As we did so, it became difficult for me to distinguish rain from perspiration on my face. My backpack swayed as my boots sank two feet deep into the snow, and for a few moments I considered the relative merits of discretion and valor. McLane, skipping rhythmically onward like a mountain goat, gazed back at me coolly. "Sorry I couldn't make it all downhill," he said, "but the Rubies just aren't that way. Don't give up," he added. "The first hour is the toughest."

I slogged on and out of the snow, and was rewarded by the appearance of the sun. We were nearing Liberty Pass at the top of the canyon, and I stopped to look back. I could see a multicolored garden of wild flowers—mountain primrose, penstemon, wyethia and others—glowing in the fresh sunlight along the stream channels. It was a scene that I had in no way anticipated in my exploration of sagebrush country—a rich, green valley flanked by forested slopes and splashed with flowers of red, blue, yellow, purple and white. The sound of a hundred rippling waterways blended with the songs of a dozen birds: thrushes, meadowlarks, finches, orioles, mountain bluebirds. Stair-stepped on the slope below me were two tiny lakes, no more than about 200 feet across, and as perfectly circular as the traditional currency of Nevada gambling casinos; appropriately, Alvin told me, they are called the Dollar Lakes. One contained mini-icebergs, turquoise in the dark green water.

A chipmunk scurried across a nearby snowfield, saw us, made a quick U-turn and retreated. In places the snow seemed to be tinted a light red, an effect created by algae of that color growing in the snow's upper layers. These microscopic plants are only a part of the fascinating spectrum of growing things that flourish in the Rubies. Botanists have counted 582 separate species in the Rubies so far, but they acknowledge that the list is incomplete. "There may be species here that no one knows about," Alvin said as we looked out over the valley. "I'd even guess there are dozens that grow here and nowhere else. It hasn't really been thoroughly studied."

A pair of fishermen appeared, making their way down from Liberty Pass. They had been fishing in one of the lakes in the mountain meadows beyond the pass, and with obvious success. "Snow's pretty thick over on that side," one told us. "It's worth it, though. There's golden trout up there just beggin' to be liberated." We thanked them, climbed past a row of boulders that guarded Liberty Pass, and stood at last at the top of the canyon—elevation 10,600 feet.

From the pass we had a wide-angle view of the effects of the ice age on the Rubies. In the history of these mountains, scientists have identified two extended periods of glaciation, one of which covered fully a third of the Rubies with ice. The glacier that carved out Lamoille Canyon was 12 miles long and more than 900 feet thick. We could readily see the results of its work: the U-shaped valley, in contrast to the V shape of conventional river-carved valleys; the deposits of till, collections of gravel and boulders left in the glacier's retreat; the steep cirque at what once was the glacial headland. The Dollar Lakes are also legacies of the departing river of ice, their perfect bowl-shaped depressions sculpted as it moved along.

The view from the other side of Liberty Pass held its own fascination in the form of three green, glittering lakes, nestled in the mountain meadows. They were much larger than the Dollars and arranged in a fairly neat line. "Liberty, Favre, Castle," Alvin intoned. Liberty Lake, its surface still dotted with floating ice in July, lay directly below us. Less than a mile beyond, at a slightly lower elevation, was Favre; the narrow meadow that separated it from Liberty looked as green as a well-tended golf course. The third lake, Castle, was perched higher than the other two, at the beginning of the rise of a towering amphitheater. "We'll camp at Liberty tonight and take a look at the other two tomorrow," Alvin said.

We descended the trail from the pass and prowled the rim of Liberty Lake until we found a reasonably sheltered site in a grove of limber pine next to a snowmelt stream. As we set up camp, Alvin was reminded of a lake story. "I don't know if it was about Liberty or not," he said, "but I like to think it was." It seems that a Shoshone chief called Sho-kup, who lived with his people in the Ruby Valley on the east side of the range, summoned a friendly white settler one day in 1861 and warned him about a "very cold lake" in the Rubies. "Here lives a big fish," Sho-kup said, "who is a very evil spirit. When he rises from the water and looks at an Indian, the Indian dies in a few days. I was at the lake and I saw the evil spirit. Now I am a very sick man." Chief Sho-kup died the next morning.

My response to this fish story was to point out that the only species we had seen in our walk around the lake were perfectly harmless and rather tasty-looking brook trout, zigzagging through the translucent water. Alvin chuckled and set about heating our freeze-dried dinner. I looked up at the sky. It was a mixture of sunset red and ominous gray; dark rain clouds were heading toward us from the west.

As we ate we watched the lake, and I remarked that this was one of the few times I had camped in the Great Basin when abundant water was actually close by. "These mountains produce more water than almost any other place in Nevada," Alvin said. He paused and listened to the wind announcing the storm to come. "I love the sound of that wind, coming from nowhere and going nowhere. It sounds so lonesome." He began to talk about his mountaineering experiences, the ascents of sheer rock cliffs and the peaks he had been the first to climb. When I asked him, inevitably, why he did it, his answer indicated careful thought. "In the old West, adventure was part of people's lives. I think adven-

A 25-foot-wide pool glistens brightly in a meadow high in the Ruby Mountains. The pool, like the larger Dollar Lakes nearby, lies in a hollow gouged out by a glacier 15,000 years ago.

ture is important, maybe necessary. But to get it today you have to fabricate your own adversity, and that's why I climb mountains."

In another hour the rain arrived, but happily it was gentle, just hard enough to pelt the roof of our nylon tent with a satisfying *pat-pat-pat.*

The next morning, as promised, Alvin took me to see Liberty's sister lakes. We stopped only briefly at Favre, just long enough for me to admire the white marsh marigolds blooming beneath the water and to spot the quick movements of trout. "Brookies," Alvin said. "The most common species in the Rubies. Those men we met yesterday got their goldens someplace else—Hidden Lake. The brookies were killed off there so that goldens could be brought in. The two don't get along together at all. The brookies breed faster and will cannibalize the goldens —so the goldens have to have isolation."

For a McLane discourse, this one was delivered in rather rapid-fire fashion, and I wondered why until I noticed him looking in the direction of Castle Lake—more specifically, at the high cirque behind it. Climbing time again, I thought, and I was right. We set out immediately, and as we approached Castle, I saw with some foreboding that the wall that served as its backdrop was prohibitively steep, a mass of granite and quartzite rising about 800 feet to the ridge line. Alvin's gaze, however, was fixed on the ridge line. "I've got to see what the view looks like on the other side," he declared. "Let's just contour up along the crest and have a look."

He scouted around and finally found an animal trail that led up a long incline toward the ridge. "This trail may be used by mountain goats," he said. "They were introduced into the Rubies by the state fish and game agency about ten years ago as an experiment, to see if they'd flourish and reproduce here. Six were brought in, and there are about thirty to fifty now. They're doing real well." I greeted this news in grim silence. I wasn't doing too well myself at the moment. After a few hundred yards the trail had disappeared under a snowfield. The going was steep and slippery, and maintaining my balance was tricky. I tried not to look down at the sharp drop-off below my left boot.

But 20 minutes later we were out of the snowfield and climbing a staircase of quartzite boulders to the ridge. The effort proved to be well worth it. The view to the east was unbroken for more than 50 miles. Ruby Valley, the broad expanse abutting the range, was a maze of shallow marshes weaving among green and long-stemmed tule bulrushes. Beyond the valley lay the long, low bulk of the Pequop Mountains, and beyond the Pequops, near the Utah-Nevada border, we could make out the hazy outline of Pilot Peak, which had been a beacon for emigrants and forty-niners.

"I wonder what those pioneers felt when they got here and saw this wall of mountains in front of them?" Alvin asked. It could not have been an encouraging sight. The Rubies, like the other ranges of the Great Basin, are much more precipitous on the east flank than on the west. I remembered my own first glimpse of the Rubies from far below on the eastern plain; their high peaks jutted up abruptly, without foothills, looming like a great city of mile-high skyscrapers. To the pioneers, this barrier must have seemed even more formidable than it did to me. Yet they persevered, and probed the approaches until they found a means of breaching the range.

The first emigrants to cross the mountains were the 33 members of the Bidwell-Bartleson caravan, who stumbled into Ruby Valley in September 1841. They were not only the first westering Americans to drive a wagon train into the Great Basin but also the first party to include females—18-year-old Nancy Kelsey and her infant daughter, Ann. Such was their ignorance of the country they were heading into that they carried boat-building equipment with them in the belief that a river flowed west from Great Salt Lake to the Pacific.

The Bidwell band got their mules and oxen through the Rubies at 7,200-foot-high Harrison Pass, and all 33 of them eventually managed to cross the Sierra Nevada and emerge into the sunshine of San Joaquin Valley. Several members of the party, in fact, became prominent Californians: Charles Weber founded the city of Stockton, Josiah Belden became the first mayor of San Jose, and John Bidwell himself received 264,133 votes as the Prohibition candidate for President in 1892. Whatever other hardships these pioneers had endured, Alvin and I agreed, a breakdown of character was not one of them.

Back at our Liberty Lake campsite late that afternoon, I was surprised to find that I had come through the day's exertions with a minimum of wear and tear. I felt invigorated, and strangely content. While Alvin was heating our dinner, I decided on another walk—a short one, to be sure. Not too far west of our camp I reached some V-shaped cuts in the mountains through which I could see the bare brown desert below. As I stood amid pines and rushing water and chirping bluebirds, and looked out at the desolate vastness of the basin, I had the feeling that I was in a secret sheltered garden peering out at the untidy world. I remembered a Nevada rancher telling me that he became "crazy for the Rubies" after weeks of working in the dry dust of the sagebrush plain. Suddenly I knew what he meant.

I returned to camp. Alvin and I ate our dinner and afterward sipped our tea in silence, watching the roseate light of the alpenglow wash the mountaintops. Then night fell, and we turned in. "By the way," Alvin said in the dark, "don't think I've forgotten your bristlecone pine." I stirred happily—then groaned. The day's climbing had taken its toll of my leg muscles after all. Alvin chuckled. "Don't worry," he said, "we'll go hunting for the bristlecone by Jeep."

The morning of my last day in the Rubies was sunny and crystal clear. My first thought, on waking, was that this was the Fourth of July; my second, that an appropriate way to celebrate would be to find a bristlecone pine. In what seemed to me to be record short order, Alvin and I retraced the trail from Liberty Pass to the base of Lamoille Canyon, retrieved the Jeep, drove down out of the mountains and re-entered them by another road some miles distant. I never did learn its name; and as things turned out, I doubt that Alvin would have wanted to have its identity—or its location—made known.

At the wheel, he seemed unusually purposeful and also unusually silent; maneuvering a car on any road in the Rubies takes close attention, and this road wound steadily upward through a long canyon that changed complexion as we climbed. Lower down it was filled with sagebrush, juniper and an occasional piñon pine. Gradually it became greener and thicker with vegetation—willows, chokecherries, mountain mahogany and aspen. The pungent aroma of sagebrush, meanwhile, gave way to the sweet fragrance of wild rose.

Alvin, intent on the road ahead, was obviously in no mood for conversation. I took advantage of the silence to let my mind rove over some facts I had read about the bristlecone pine. Certainly it would never be found in the kind of landscape we were passing through; invariably, it grows on rocky, windswept slopes where the soil is shallow and the water relatively meager. Adversity itself seems to help the tree create its means of survival. The slower it grows in its dry environment, the more resinous it becomes; in turn, the chemical properties of the resin help ward off decay and insect damage, thus prolonging the bristlecone's life.

Beside the life-prolonging resin, the tree also benefits from the extraordinary durability of its foxtail-shaped bunches of needles. These serve the same function as leaves, manufacturing the tree's essential nu-

A bristlecone pine, twisted by nearly 2,000 years of buffeting by winds, snow and ice, stands defiantly atop a crumbling rocky slope high on a Nevada mountain. Perfectly adapted to the severe climate at such altitudes, bristlecone pines are the oldest living things on earth. Trunk borings have showed some specimens to be 4,000 years old; and the climatologic history of the region is written in their growth rings: drought years produce narrow rings and wet years leave wide ones.

trients through photosynthesis. The needles frequently stay on for 20 or 30 years, far longer than most other pine needles. This means that a bristlecone can withstand a succession of years of drought, when fewer needles are produced.

Alvin's voice brought me back to our surroundings. "Look at the carvings on those aspen," he said. There were several groves of them, perhaps 50 trees to a grove, and the soft white bark of every one of them was carved with words and pictures—a house, an American flag, men on horseback, women's faces. This canyon had been periodically grazed by sheep, and the sheepherders, most of them Basques who worked the flocks for a few years and then returned to their homeland, had left a record of inscriptions behind them.

We paused for a better look. Most of the carvings included the herder's name and a date. Some of the dates went back more than 50 years. Inscriptions ran to whole sentences. Alvin commented that they had even been the subject of a research paper. The researcher had found that they very often dealt with women. *El que tiene que estar aqui esta medio loco porque no tiene una puta,* one carving read—"he who has to be here must be half crazy because he has no woman."

The Jeep climbed still higher, passing little clearings filled with flame-colored Indian paintbrush, scarlet columbine and elaborate, mound-shaped beaver houses. Beaver-felled trees lay across one another in piles. In one sylvan glade we saw a red-tailed hawk hanging head down from a branch of a dead aspen, its wings outspread; somehow they had gotten tangled in the branches just above. The bird fluttered, trying to get free, as we watched. In a moment its mate appeared, screeching as it cruised over the dead tree. In another moment the upside-down hawk managed to unsnarl itself; it dropped about five feet, clumsily righted itself and flew off with its mate.

In a few more minutes we were out of the green forests and meadows and riding along an exposed rocky ridge with the silver strands of the streams and man-made canals of the Ruby Marsh wildlife refuge glimmering far below us to the southeast. Our elevation was now near 9,000 feet. The road continued across a pass and up another ridge, requiring a shift into four-wheel drive. There were no birds to be seen, and only a few limber pines.

Bristlecone territory, I thought, and at that instant Alvin slammed on the brakes. "There they are—look over there!" he cried. Just below the summit I saw a scattered grove of eerie-looking trees. They were perhaps 10 to 30 feet high, squat and thick trunked. The trunks jutted every which way; the branches angled off asymmetrically, seeming to grope outward in a kind of arboreal anguish. The bark of some trees was polished to a smooth, jewel-like gloss—no doubt by centuries of blowing ice and snow. Several downed bristlecones lay heavily and mournfully on the ground, like fallen warriors. Others, perhaps four-fifths dead, still stood, their only lifeline a thin ribbon of bark protecting the living tissue that remained beneath. Most of the survivors, however, seemed to be flourishing, their multiple twisted trunks striped with hundreds of narrow rings, their branches laden with needle bunches—foxtail shaped, just as I had read.

We had no way of estimating with any accuracy how old these bristlecones were. That involved an analysis of their growth rings; interestingly enough, Alvin said, examination of the rings appears to be more accurate a measure of age than radiocarbon testing. In any event, the need for precise accuracy seemed somehow irrelevant. "Put it this way," Alvin suggested. "Some of these trees were old when Christ was born." And, I thought, they were around at a time when civilization as we know it emerged from its primitive origins to whatever dubious glory it enjoys today.

We stood on the summit for a while, looking at the grove of bristlecones and past them, past the flowered meadows and on to the valleys on either side. Then we got into the Jeep for the ride back down. Alvin seemed preoccupied. The reason became apparent when we said good-bye several hours later in Elko. "If you have to tell anybody about that place," he said earnestly, "at least make it sound a little difficult for them." At my look of surprise, he relented a little. "Well, at least as far as the litterbugs are concerned. The fewer of them that go in, the better off the Rubies will be."

NATURE WALK / On Wheeler Peak

PHOTOGRAPHS AND TEXT BY DAVID CAVAGNARO

Wheeler Peak in northeastern Nevada's Snake Range rises 13,063 feet from a base on the desert floor to a glacier-sculptured summit. Lakes lie tucked in its rocky pockets and streams slice its flanks. On a bright, crisp September day, photographer-naturalist David Cavagnaro and a companion, Tom Binger, hiked from Stella Lake, at 11,000 feet, down eight miles of trails to the edge of an ancient terminal moraine overlooking the desert. The dawn-to-dusk walk took the men into four distinct zones of vegetation, each characterized by certain dominant trees and plants. The text that follows is drawn from the notes that Cavagnaro made during the day's hike.

Not long after dawn broke over windswept Wheeler Peak, we stood on the shore of Stella Lake about 2,000 feet below the summit. The air temperature was below freezing —28° F.—but the sun's warming rays soon melted the ice around the lake's margins as a few aquatic beetles skimmed through the chill waters. Formed by a glacier and fed by springs and melting snow, the lake had grown shallower during the summer. Now it was only three feet deep; it would soon be frozen solid, all life stilled until spring.

Surrounding us was a forest of limber pine with some Engelmann spruce interspersed. Beneath our feet, breaking through the thin layer of soil, was a cracked pavement of quartzite shattered by frost action into slabs and chips that were tinted green, gray and blue. The coloration, we later learned, was from minerals in the natural cement that bound the grains of sand together when this now-fragmented rock was metamorphosed from sandstone millions of years ago. Among the colorful rocks, spruce and pine needles and cones that had been blown into crevices by the wind looked like grout in a giant abstract mosaic.

Here and there large mats of mountain juniper spread their creeping boughs across the paving stones. In some places the juniper boughs embraced old gray or reddish stumps of dead trees that had become marked with the holes and glyphs of wood engravers, boring beetles that seek shelter and sustenance in trees. No living trace of the beetles was to be found, for there was nothing left here to feed them. They usually bore between the bark and wood, often destroying the cambium tissue and killing the tree. Whether the beetles had caused the deaths of these trees, we could not determine.

Close to the lake shore there were patches of greenery—bunch grass, dock, fleabane and other species of low-growing plants long past blooming, their dry seed heads rustling gently in the morning breeze.

Below Stella Lake the trail entered

DEAD JUNIPER BRANCHES

great stands of silver-trunked, color-splashed aspen, interspersed with pines and spruces, that spread out across the mountainside. Entering the grove, I had the impression of walking into a sylvan rainbow, for at Wheeler the aspen in fall take on many hues beyond the yellow gold familiar in many parts of the country. Here they blaze with the variety of an Eastern hardwood forest.

On this particular morning, groves of trees with leaves turned red and

LIMBER PINE ON THE SHORES OF STELLA LAKE

even burgundy seemed to burn among the more common brilliant yellow. Spotted among them were stands turned pumpkin orange. The various colors are genetically determined, with each different hue appearing on distinct groups of trees, called clones, having common root systems. The red strain, once com-

GRAPE AND ASPEN LEAVES

paratively rare, seems to be spreading on the slopes of Wheeler and elsewhere in the West.

District Ranger Jack Wilcox had told us the day before that the aspen were especially brilliant this year, a fact he attributed to a drought that had settled over the area in April. During droughts, night temperatures are usually milder and severe frosts are consequently uncommon. Heavy frost causes the adhesion layer between the leaf and the branch to freeze, shutting off all water and thus killing the leaf—which turns yellowish brown and falls.

AN ASPEN GROVE BENEATH THE SUMMIT

RED ROOTS OF WILLOW IN LEHMAN CREEK

MOSS ON QUARTZITE CHIPS IN THE CREEK BED

When only light frosts occur, however, the leaves fully develop their color, dying and falling gradually as the tree shuts down for winter.

Adding to the color of the aspen was the deep glow of low-growing Oregon grape. This hardy shrub is common to alpine glades in this part of the West, and its high tolerance for shade enables it to thrive among dense stands of aspen. The Oregon grape maintains most of its leaves throughout the winter, their color changing from dark green to red at the approach of cold weather. In the spring the red leaves drop and are replaced by new green foliage. The plants we saw were dwarfed versions of the Oregon grape: they also differ in often having only two or three leaf clusters rather than the usual five to nine.

A Mountainside Stream

As we passed through the aspen grove, Lehman Creek swirled by the trail. Surprisingly, it was little reduced by the drought, and was running clear and cold. The underground water table, well-supplied by a heavy snowfall the previous winter, still held an ample reserve to keep the creek bubbling.

The moisture from the creek and the plants along its margins attracted a number of insects. A few lively butterflies—painted ladies, a morning cloak, and a monarch—flitted by. One casualty was a drowned white-lined sphinx moth we saw floating

A SPHINX MOTH AFLOAT

on thin, elongated leaves of aquatic grass mixed with Engelmann-spruce seeds and other flotsam on the creek surface. It had probably died during the night. Daylight is a quiet time for sphinx moths; they become most active at dusk. Swift, tireless fliers that can dart at speeds up to 35 miles an hour, the moths are often mistaken for hummingbirds as they hover on vibrating wings in front of flower blossoms. At rest the moths extend their wings to display the protective coloration and patterning that gives them the look of bark or dry leaves.

Along the creek's edge hung the remnants of spring and summer growth. In some places the narrow red roots of willow trees trailed in the riffles of limpid water. Floating just beneath the surface, atop a bed of quartzite chips and looking like a scattered colony of centipedes were strands of aquatic moss.

We had been descending through

the forest for about five hours when the landscape opened up—the big trees and their shade were left behind. The sun blazed hot upon us as we paused to have our lunch.

Shrubs as Big as Trees

All around us stretched a dwarfed forest of mountain mahogany. This plant, with its tough, twisted branches, was called mahogany by settlers in the West because of its hard reddish wood, but it is unrelated to the towering mahogany of the tropics. Indeed, mountain mahogany is not strictly speaking even a tree. A member of the rose family, it grows up in several trunks or stems and is thus formally classified as a shrub— although it may achieve heights of over 20 feet. We later discovered that the largest mountain mahogany recorded anywhere in the world grows only a short distance from our trail. Some 13 feet in circumference at its base, it is about 28 feet tall. We saw many along our way that were nearly that high.

The park naturalist believes that the unusual height of the mahogany on Wheeler is due to the good depth of soil and plentiful moisture. They are also larger because they have never been cut, and hence are older. At other places in the West, the mahogany has been cut for firewood; its hard logs produce an especially hot flame, and miners used to prefer it to coal in their smelters because the wood was so accessible, and therefore cheap. Although mining has been done on Wheeler, there was no smelting.

The trees we passed on this

FLOWERING RABBITBRUSH BENEATH MOUNTAIN MAHOGANY

stretch of the trail had partly taken on their autumn color but kept their foliage. This is characteristic of mountain mahogany, which loses, at most, about 25 per cent of its leaves. Those that fall do not change color until just before they drop, when they abruptly turn from a deep green to brownish yellow. Many of the trees we saw were also covered with seeds topped by white plumes up to two inches long.

Among the mountain-mahogany shrubs and sagebrush we saw our first rabbitbrush, with golden flowers blooming as though there had been no drought. The reason, we later learned, is that the rabbitbrush's long taproots can draw moisture from far below the surface.

As we strolled among the rocks and bunch grasses on the slopes, we found a yellow-jacket nest built securely in a sagebrush near the trail. The insects were busily flying in and out, but fortunately we discovered the nest before the yellow jackets discovered us. Here, too, squirrels and chipmunks had been at work among the cones fallen from the spruce and now lying among the mahogany. On a toppled mahogany trunk were cores of cones, testimony to the rodents' foraging.

As we descended farther down the valley of Lehman Creek, the vegetation changed again. Thickets of chokecherry were growing just back of the stream banks, their leaves turning scarlet. We sampled a few of the purple fruits that hung from the branches in clusters and found them astringent but refreshing.

GNAWED CORES OF SPRUCE CONES

YELLOW-JACKET NEST ON SAGEBRUSH

WESTERN CHOKECHERRY BERRIES

PIÑON PINE ON A ROCKY SLOPE

At 8,000 feet we left behind the last of the mountain mahoganies and encountered stands of single-leaf piñon pine and Utah juniper. Beyond the foothills that harbor the last of the conifers stretch the vast expanses of desert that lie between the ranges surrounding Wheeler Peak. There, below 6,000 feet, the heat and the aridity are too much even for the adaptable pines.

A Pine-Nut Harvest

The piñon pines here at the margin were at the height of their seed-producing activity. Every tree was burdened with an enormous crop of cones that had recently opened, revealing the oval nuts. These were not only edible but delicious.

At first we stripped off the thin, coarse brown shells before eating the white meat of the nuts. The oily flesh was so tasty, however, that we quickly abandoned the tedious job of shelling and began consuming them by the handful, shells and all. The shells tasted slightly bitter, like the inside covering of a peanut. But we were not put off our feast. There was one inconvenience, however: our hands became coated with the sticky pitch that covers the cones.

Pine nuts have extraordinary nutritional value: there are 3,000 calories to a pound. They are much prized by Navajo and other Indian cooks as well as by organic-food lovers and gourmet cooks. So they are harvested both commercially and by some individuals. Commercial pickers must obtain a permit from the Forest Service or the Bureau of Land Management and pay five cents a

NUTS IN A PIÑON-PINE CONE

RIPE BERRIES OF A UTAH JUNIPER

FLOWER-LIKE GALLS ON A JUNIPER

MIDGE-FLY GALLS ON SAGEBRUSH

pound for their harvest. Amateur nutpickers also require a permit, but they pay no fee, and they are limited to 25 pounds. Humans are not the only harvesters of these nuts. Opened cones and chewed shells littered the ground beneath the pines we walked through—more evidence of winter food storage by the busy squirrels and chipmunks.

Other rodents had discovered the succulent and decorative fruits of the Utah juniper as well. The junipers were heavily laden with small silver berries, and the ground beneath the shrubby trees was strewn with partly eaten and now rotting remnants of the fruit. From the look of it, mice had apparently been gnawing on the dropped berries.

Fascinated by an old, gnarled juniper (they grow to a height of 10 to 15 feet), I climbed it, whereupon I discovered some peculiar green and brown rosettes. Growing like flowers among the juniper twigs, they were insect galls, an ingenious device by which an insect's eggs, laid within a plant's tissues, are protected. The plant reacts to a chemical secreted by the insect at the time the eggs are laid and simply grows around the insect larvae. The gall remains green until it finishes its growth cycle, whereupon it dies and turns brown. The insects that had produced these unusual juniper galls, I subsequently found out, were midge flies.

As we left the juniper grove, we came upon the shelflike edge of the terminal moraine on Wheeler's flank. Beneath us, at approximately 7,000 feet, stretched a gently sloping alluvial fan, which is still being formed when the torrential runoff from seasonal rains washes gravel and fragmented boulders out of the moraine. The formation is so porous that it engulfs the last piece of Lehman Creek, which vanishes to run underground into the desert.

Clumps of autumn asters and stands of silvery narrow-leafed willow grew out of the gravelly soil. On the stems of sagebrush nearby we spotted a gray-green version of the midge-fly galls.

Fuzzy bee flies, which both look and behave remarkably like bees but actually are members of the fly family, were flitting from place to place. They would hover briefly over a rabbitbrush flower, poking their long proboscises inside to suck nectar, or they would rest for a moment on the rocky ground. Like the sphinx moth,

CRESTED WHEAT-GRASS SEEDS

A BEE FLY RESTING ON QUARTZITE

bee flies are speedy fliers that can hover in midair. Unlike the twilight-loving moths, however, bee flies gather nectar by daylight from flowers in warm, sunny spots.

As we paused to do some insect watching, our eyes were drawn to the plants that the flies seemed to favor. Colorful rabbitbrush shrubs formed a golden carpet between the piñons. Tough clumps of crested wheat grass erupted from place to place, their symmetrical tops looking like the feathered ends of arrows. But it was the rabbitbrush that formed the main center of insect activity because it was the only flowering plant in bloom.

Now as the sun sank toward the ridge of Wheeler Peak behind us, its fading rays picked out yet one more brilliant red patch of Oregon grape, growing here at the edge of the desert as confidently as it does among the high aspen. The sunshine rapidly retreated from the alluvial fan, and we clambered up onto a pine-covered ridge to catch the dying rays. When the sun finally abandoned even this high promontory, a chill gripped the land. We sat beneath a twisted piñon, watching the long, dark shadow of Wheeler Peak creep across the sagebrush-speckled desert below us. Looking out toward the north, we saw 12,050-foot Mount Moriah, a smaller counterpart of Wheeler Peak and about 20 miles away as the crow flies. Finally, even Mount Moriah was swallowed up in shadow, and the eastern horizon glowed with the pastel pink and blue of desert twilight.

MOUNT MORIAH JUST BEFORE SUNSET

4/ Black Rock Journal

*People came, and passed by... the spring and the meadow
and the hummocks and the black rock that
looms above — the place remained. They could not change it.
It was too strong for them.* GEORGE R. STEWART/ *SHEEP ROCK*

Alvin McLane and I zipped across the hard-packed playa—the flat basin bottom—of the Black Rock Desert in his bright red Jeep. It was
morning of the longest day of the year. He was to deposit me at Black
Rock Spring, at the base of the massive outcrop that gives the area its
name. I would be camping alone on the fringe of this northwestern Nevada desert, hoping to gain some feel for the solitary life of the settler
in this hard country, possibly even a sense of what the pioneers who
had passed through it had felt. According to Alvin, the place looked so
much the way it did when people first saw it that it would be ideal for
my purposes. Three days hence, barring any of the various calamities
now skidding through my mind, Alvin would return to pick me up.

I felt both an eager anticipation and a sense of dread, and at the moment the latter was gaining. What if something happened to Alvin and
he couldn't return in three days? What if a rare summer cloudburst
turned the playa into an impassable lake, as often happened in the winter? Black Rock, after all, was inaccessible three or four months of the
year, when snowmelt turned it into a mud flat. What if I foolishly got
myself lost, or fell while climbing and broke a bone? On the previous
evening I had prudently consulted a fortune cookie at a Chinese res-
taurant in Reno, 120 miles to the southwest. "You will travel to many
places," it promised. I took that to mean I would survive Black Rock.

Ahead I could see a long reddish-brown range of mountains, diminishing gradually in elevation from north to south, and at its southern end, seemingly standing apart, a single black rock perhaps 500 feet high. From a distance the rock resembled a bear sleeping on its side.

The Jeep rode smoothly over the hard and level alkali surface. The playa's color was a combination of gray, brown and yellow, with gray predominating. The horizon was so flat that a small but gritty saltbush, alone on a tiny mound, was visible a couple of miles away.

"What if it rains and you can't get through to retrieve me?" I asked as matter-of-factly as I could.

"Those overnight lakes dry up as fast as they form," Alvin replied. "It wouldn't hold me up more than a day." He paused. "That's not what you have to worry about anyway," he said, then lapsed into silence.

I contained myself for perhaps 60 seconds. "Well, what *should* I worry about?"

"A rattler bite or scorpion sting," he said calmly, "but you'll be all right if you just look carefully at any shady places before you put a hand or foot there. If you get bitten by a rattler just put a tourniquet above the swelling."

"What if I get lost?"

"Don't see how you can. You'll be at Black Rock Point, and that's the biggest landmark for 50 miles around." He smiled. "Pretty hard to lose it." I must have looked confused, for he explained that the rock itself is properly designated Black Rock Point, and appears that way on maps.

We reached the base of the mountains and entered an area of hummocks, each one topped by a spiny, green-leafed greasewood bush. Alvin nosed the Jeep around until he found an old trail through the mounds. We turned onto it. "This is part of the Applegate Trail," he said, explaining that in 1846 a pioneer named Jesse Applegate had been directed by Oregon settlers to carve out a new trail to the Willamette Valley. Alvin glanced around cheerfully, suddenly animated. "How about this?" he said. "Lonely enough for you?" He spread an arm toward the immense treeless playa. "I don't know many places where you can feel isolation the way you can here."

Our trail meandered among the hummocks that lay between the Black Rock Range and the flat alkali plain. After a few minutes we saw a good-sized meadow of tall bulrushes and salt grass, brilliantly green against the desert and pale blue sky. We stopped at a dark pool of water, about 20 feet in diameter, between the meadow and the trail. Thin strands of steam rose from the hot water. We were at Black Rock Spring.

We unloaded my provisions and pitched a canvas tent. I had food enough for five or six days and a half-dozen gallons of water. I dug a fire pit and surrounded it with some rocks that had washed down from Black Rock. Then I began gathering dead greasewood branches.

Alvin watched my progress with interest, then climbed into the Jeep. "You sweat a lot," he observed. "Don't forget to use your salt."

I finished the housekeeping chores and made a preliminary reconnaissance of my campsite. The pitted black bulk of the rock, its slopes strewn with charcoal-colored slabs and boulders, was a few hundred yards to the east. A line of greasewood-covered hummocks started just past the spring and ran northeast to the mountains. Another colony of hummocks—which turned out to be mounds of vegetation about five feet high—filled the area between my tent and the desert. To the southwest I could see the hazy outlines of the Granite Range, broken by a gap. The Y-shaped Black Rock Desert, one of the world's largest playas, begins near that gap and stretches northeast in two corridors that extend on either side of the Black Rock Range, each about 90 miles long and up to 20 miles wide. The floor of this vast alkali plain is 4,000 feet above sea level.

The gap appeared to be filled with a low blue haze that cut off the base of the bordering mountains. The lower slopes seemed to curl above the fog, which I now realized was a mirage. I had read that oxen brought here by pioneers had stampeded into the desert toward what looked like water; and I knew that heat waves had bewitched human travelers as well. One longtime explorer of the Black Rock region had told me of a time when he rode several miles toward what appeared to be a sizable hill topped by a pine tree, only to reach it and discover a five-foot mound crowned by a stumpy greasewood.

I could see a low cloud of dust trailing the Jeep halfway across the desert, but nothing else stirred in the shimmering afternoon heat—it was in the 90s—except large horseflies evidently welcoming a warm-blooded creature. I turned to my camp, home for the next three days.

A few yards from my tent was the shell of an old wagon; its cloth cover was gone but the wooden frame appeared intact and unmarred. Alvin had told me that it had been abandoned long ago by a sheep-herder. Its wheels had disappeared and the wagon bed, above which arched weathered wooden ribs, now rested on the ground. The wagon served as the man's home as well as his transportation, and his small "front door" still banged when the wind blew. Nearby were the remains of a campfire and a pile of .22-caliber shells. The wagon had

A Black Rock Desert pool is colored by algae nourished by water from a hot spring. The water temperature ranges from 165° to 191° F.

been there, I later learned, for at least 40 years, yet no one had torn it up for firewood. More surprisingly, no one had left his initials on its frame—the surest possible evidence of its (and my) isolation. But why had the herder left it? Was he trapped in a blizzard? The victim of a range feud? Perhaps the wagon was damaged and not worth the trouble of repairing. Perhaps the herder himself had decided the wheels were worth saving, and had taken them along when he left.

Black Rock Spring was a few yards away. It was green-brown and dark. Bulrushes surrounded it save for one open space on the side nearest the trail. It emitted an odor of hot sulfur, bespeaking its volcanic origin. I inserted a finger in the water and withdrew it—the temperature, I learned later, was 136° F. Salt grass extended several hundred yards below the spring, sloping gently toward the playa. I could see a few small birds, larks and phoebes darting amid the bulrushes, and insects swarmed everywhere. A collared lizard, so named because of the twin dark bands around its neck, scooted across the grass beside me. This pool was the only source of water within a radius of some 10 miles, and what life there was in this inhospitable place—grass, insects and birds—was clustered here. I noticed several animal dens, shallow holes perhaps 15 inches in diameter, in the cleared area on the edge of the hot spring. The four-legged residents—they could have been coyotes, foxes or badgers—were out of sight.

I knew that pioneers on the Applegate Trail had camped here. The travelers cut northwest from the main California trail at the Humboldt River and followed a route of day-long treks between springs. "It was a country which had nothing of a redeeming character," one 1846 diarist complained. "It seemed to be the River of Death dried up, and having its muddy bottom jetted into cones by the force of the fires of perdition. It was enlivened by the murmur of no streams, but was a wide waste of desolation."

It was a trail rimmed with agony. Thirsty oxen bolted from the trains and leaped into hot springs, where they were scalded to death. Horses dropped from exhaustion and thirst. One pioneer, George Riddle, noted in his 1851 diary that his predecessors had strewn the trail with some of their most cherished possessions when it became necessary to lighten their wagons. He saw jettisoned feather beds, cookstoves, plows and—almost miraculous that it had survived *that* far—a melodeon.

I could imagine the arrival at the spring of the first emigrants, bleary with thirst and exhaustion. They would have shouted for joy and leaped down from their wagons, racing for the water. Horses and oxen would follow them to the edge of the dark pool. Then the first child to reach it would dip his hands in, shout with surprise and run to his mother. After a while they would discover the spring's overflow pool, barely cool enough to drink, in the reedy grass.

My ears were becoming accustomed to the stillness, and the whirring horseflies now seemed as loud as a lawn mower. It was mid-afternoon, and the blue blanket of the mirage had moved a little higher up the sides of the distant peaks. On the desert floor I saw a picket line of dust devils, cyclone-shaped swirls of alkali dust, whipped crazily around by the wind. There were great cracks in the baked mud that gave it the appearance of a loosely assembled jigsaw puzzle.

Walking toward the playa along the edge of the meadow, I was surprised to come upon pieces of wire fencing and weathered fence posts. Farther on I passed an old wooden gate. The ground was littered with broken glass, rusted metal, even a length of iron pipe. I realized these were the remains of an old cabin: someone, sometime, had actually lived here. Scattered amid the debris of this settler were older artifacts —bits of black obsidian and butterscotch-colored jasper, arrowheads and spear points and chipping tools used by Indians. How many people, how many years apart, had tried to live at Black Rock Spring? The Indian chips were the remnants of one such attempt, the settler's cabin was another, the sheepherder's wagon a third. It occurred to me that the artifacts of two cultures shared a common overlay of aggressiveness —the Indians' spear points, the campers' .22 shells.

I decided to explore the cabin's ruins later, so I returned to my campsite and set about cooking dinner—steak barbecued on a grill improvised from a piece of metal I found. The sun was still fairly high above the red-brown Calico Mountains to the west, and for the first time I became conscious of the breadth of the sky. Dark clouds were moving down from the north, and another line of low clouds lay below the sun in the west. It seemed to me that I could see 100 miles. Rain was falling on a ridge farther up the Black Rock Range. I knew that the desert floor receives no more than five inches of precipitation a year, as snow and summer rain. In the mountains a few thousand feet higher, the annual rainfall is more than twice that.

The scope of the horizon made it possible to see weather form, to see clouds mass and drift and disperse. Alvin had told me about winter fogs in Black Rock that turned the desert into a vast, billowing ocean dotted with islands—the mountains.

The sun dipped behind the Calicos and the horseflies settled down for the night, to be replaced by mosquitoes. I sat in the cooling evening and watched the glow of sunset spread 270° around the horizon, blocked only by the looming black presence of the rock. Shortly after nine the first star popped out, and within an hour the sky was laced with the jewels of night. I curled my hand in front of my eye like a telescope and counted stars within the circle of my fist until I had to stop.

George R. Stewart, a student of Western history and the author of a semifictional description of Black Rock, tells the story of two Nevada ranchers discussing a night when they had watched in fascination and horror as stars seemed to fall all over the sky.

"Did you see the stars a-fallin'?" one asks.

"Sure did," the other replies.

"Bad down our way!" the first one says. "Two stars has fell outta the dipper, and the Milky Way's all *shot to hell.*"

I counted four falling stars before I crawled into my tent.

In the morning I packed a small cloth bag with two oranges, binoculars and a topographic map and set out to climb the rock. I headed first for a saddle about 200 feet above the north base of the slope. This was not so much a climb as a scramble over gravel and moderate-sized boulders. A pair of croaking ravens cruised by me and flew on toward the meadow in search of breakfast. I remembered that an 1849 diarist had reported so many crows and ravens at Black Rock that he surmised it was a rookery. It isn't. In that Gold Rush year, though, the traffic of wagons and animals past Black Rock Spring was heavier than at any other time before or since, and many animals died in the desert. The bird population had undoubtedly increased with the scavenging opportunities.

From the saddle I had my first view of the country east of the rock. The desolate gray-brown playa stretched on to the Jackson Mountains, dimly visible in the distance. I saw nothing moving and little growing. A shallow groove in the desert headed southeast and disappeared into the playa—the pioneer trail, still visible after a century of disuse.

I slipped and stumbled from boulder to boulder up the talus slope above the saddle. Much of the gravel was as dark as coal. The rock was like a landmark in hell, black and barren and devoid of life. The rocks on its slopes were like fragments of cinder, splintered by frost action. Frémont had described this rock as a "jagged broken point, bare and torn," and there was indeed something distinctively bleak about it. Large boulders marked the course of summer-dry washes on the fairly

An eight-month-old coyote surveys his new domain on a January morning. Born in spring, coyote cubs leave their native territories in the fall, forced out by parents unsure of sufficient winter food for themselves. Cubs have been known to migrate more than 100 miles from their birthplaces in search of favorable hunting grounds.

steep upper slope. I stepped carefully across a ledge to get around a protruding rock and was momentarily alarmed when the rock I was clinging to broke off in my hand. A true mountaineer could have made this climb on a bicycle, but it was nonetheless satisfying to ascend one last boulder and find myself at the top.

The meadow below me looked like a small green garden eccentrically dropped on the desert. A small circular playa lay to the northeast just below the nearest peak. It looked like a perfect little lake without its water, which of course is just what it was.

From my vantage point at its top I was all the more impressed by the origins of Black Rock itself. Most of this area was covered by sea 250 million years ago, when the underlying material of Black Rock was formed: andesite, spewed up through faults during volcanic eruptions; and limestone, the remains of sea creatures. As the eons passed, new rock was formed over the old. During a period of major faulting 30 or 40 million years ago, the Black Rock Range was formed. Lesser faulting in one area—at Black Rock—raised the older rock higher than the newer, and subsequent erosion over the years exposed it.

The desert itself owes its character to a much younger phenomenon on the geologic clock: the prehistoric Lake Lahontan, which at its peak covered Black Rock Desert with 500 feet of water. Lahontan's rise corresponded with that of Lake Bonneville in the eastern Great Basin, during the last ice age.

Bonneville had been a great shapeless expanse peppered with islands, but Lahontan's shoreline was a quirky network of long inlets and narrow, fjordlike bays weaving among the peaks. What had it been like? I could imagine sailing down long, narrow corridors of blue water, looking up at the pine forests on the bordering peaks and seeing above the trees the silver-white and glittering glacier. Large animals —bears, elk, mountain sheep—would have been visible through the trees. Where one now sees a world of gray-white alkali dust and sand there had been deep blues, forest greens, and the rich reds, yellows and violets of wild flowers.

By about 7,500 years ago the lake was completely gone, except for the few remnants like Pyramid (75 miles southwest of Black Rock). During the long twilight of evaporation the character of the country changed dramatically. Gone with the glaciers were not only the lake but also the evergreens, the forest animals, the lush undergrowth and the sweet grasslands. New communities of life replaced the old. They were hardier, more tolerant—sagebrush and juniper, antelope and mule deer. But, in time, even they passed on, routed by the harshness of Black Rock Desert.

And finally there were only the survivors, the toughest of all, those that endure where even sagebrush and juniper cannot. They are there yet, living at the playa's edge: coyote, kangaroo rat, kit fox and raven, greasewood, shad scale and pickleweed—the last desperate line of defense, those fortified against barrenness, those that have adapted.

As the lake dried, some of its salt was buried under eroded silt, mud and clay, from which the surface of the desert was formed. Now only rain and snowmelt can revive the lake for a fitful day or two before its shallow expanse once again yields to the relentless sun. The low blue haze of its afternoon mirage seems almost a ghost of the desert's past.

From the summit of Black Rock it was easy to imagine that I was on an island in the long-dead lake, with waves washing the boulders below me. I was ready to descend, but before I left I celebrated my presence there by building a small cairn and inserting a page of notebook paper containing my name and hometown and the date.

I scrambled down the slope and hiked northeast toward the little playa I had seen from the summit. I was now headed directly away from my campsite and into the Black Rock Range. The playa was separated from the desert by a long incline that rose perhaps a hundred feet above the level of my campsite. I crossed a band of desert pavement —so called because of its similarity to cobblestones—a thin layer of burnished pebbles, fitted together by wind and water as if they had been cemented in place. Nearby I found an empty shell cartridge about six inches long, a reminder that this area was a gunnery range for naval aircraft during World War II. Just then, as if to underline the unnatural intrusion represented by the shell, a sonic boom split the air around me. Its echoes rippled along the mountainside. I looked up, but could not see the plane.

I reached the little playa and saw that it was in a perfect bowl perhaps two miles around. In the Rockies or Sierra it would have been a dark lake, glistening with fish and surrounded by pines. But here it was a basin of alkali dust, hosting only pickleweed plants.

The morning sun was well up by now and I headed back along the side of Black Rock to find shade on the western slope. My earlier apprehensions had fled, and I was suddenly aware that I was enjoying the solitude of this place and even beginning to feel proprietary about it.

I settled back against a shaded boulder on the west side of the rock,

Hummocks of dried mud in Nevada's Black Rock Desert pick up the reflected glow of sunset from cirrus clouds overhead.

overlooking my camp and the desert beyond. I savored the thought that every minute here was my own, utterly, to spend any way I pleased. Time passed so slowly here. There were no pressures, no deadlines. The sense of time seemed related to the vast expanse of uncluttered space. Each seemed to complement the other: the leisurely passage of time made possible an appreciation of space, of land and sky, and of the rare and exciting signs of life; the quiet reach of the land, in turn, imposed a stately rhythm on the hours.

It seems paradoxical that a place of such infinite dimensions should make one more conscious of detail, but it does. One's senses always sharpen in wilderness; in the desert particularly they seem to be at their most acute. Perhaps it is because there are so few distractions, or it may be that one's primitive instincts for survival recognize any alien sight or sound as potentially dangerous.

Alvin McLane had told me of a turn-of-the-century writer who felt that some lands should be permanently set aside not for their recreational potential nor even their physical beauty, but because they evoke "Silence, and Space, and the Great Winds." The meaning of that phrase was becoming clear to me, as the sun pierced the last alcove of shade on my mountainside. I set off for the tent and its flimsy protection against the strong winds and searing heat of the afternoon.

I was adapting my own activity to the daily cycle of the desert. I had rapidly discovered that morning and evening, before and after the inevitable onslaughts of sun and wind, were the best times to explore. In the afternoon, when the sun pounded down relentlessly and the hard, hot wind blew off the desert, I had a strong impulse to hibernate. It was too hot to walk very far, and I was mindful of McLane's observation that I perspired readily and needed to be alert to the loss of body salt. I had brought two books about the Black Rock area along with me: *Sheep Rock* and a history of the Applegate Trail. I ate a light lunch and retired to the tent to read, but after a couple of hours I became irritated with the tent's constant flapping in the wind and ventured outside again, searching for a greasewood bush large enough to provide a patch of shade. I finally found a spot that offered about three feet of midafternoon shade against the westering sun. The main liability of this site was that I had to share it with a swarm of aggressive horseflies. It was, nevertheless, the best solution I could come up with, and I leaned back against the wall of a hummock to read until dinnertime.

The solitude I had come to treasure persisted through my first full day and a half at Black Rock Spring—which surprised me. This was the first weekend of summer and I had half-expected, half-feared that I would encounter rock hounds, Indian-chip collectors or truck campers. My first and only company turned out to be none of these.

I had arrived on midday Friday and climbed the rock on Saturday morning. Now it was Sunday morning, and I was trying (unsuccessfully) to hard-boil an egg in the hot spring water, when I heard the unmistakable sound of an approaching car. In a few minutes two men drove up in a Jeep and stopped. I walked over.

"Enjoying it out here?" the driver asked. Slightly startled by the sound of my own voice, I replied that I liked it fine.

The other man shook his head. "Sure is desolate," he said. "See any snakes?" I said I hadn't. We talked for a few minutes. They told me that they were doing geothermal research on a grant from the National Science Foundation. They were trying to locate underground hot-water conduits that might eventually be useful as sources of energy.

As the driver started the motor he looked at me skeptically, but managed a polite, "Well, stay out of trouble." I waved as the Jeep bounced on down the trail.

I spent most of the morning taking a long walk around the spring and along the edge of the playa. From the west, or desert, side of the spring the view of the rock itself was stunning. I looked across the meadow of green salt grass and bulrushes to the pitted, shiny blackness of the rock. I was struck with an impression of rich and deep colors—the green meadow, the ebony rock and the blue sky.

In the afternoon I abandoned my books and returned to the settler's cabin I had discovered soon after my arrival. A few yards from the remains of the main cabin I found a smaller, rectangular bed of ashes —the remains of a shed, perhaps. Pieces of wire on the ground suggested some kind of animal pen—did he keep chickens? A child's shoe poked out of the ashes—a family lived here. I began to dig carefully through the ashes with my knife, uncovering nails, pieces of brown and green glass, parts of dishes, metal cans of all sizes. The temptation to speculate was irresistible. How long did they live here? What brought them here? Were they marooned in the winter? How did the fire start?

Long lengths of pipe indicated that the settlers had piped water from the spring to the cabin. They probably had to let it cool before they could drink it. I found a brass button and a small metal hook in the ashes, remnants of the settlers' clothing. Did that mean that the fire had caught them by surprise, before they could empty their closets, or while they were away? Buried in the ashes were several six-inch-long pieces of what looked and felt like blackened chalk. Did they have a blackboard for home tutoring? The archeological evidence suggested a hasty exit—dishes, clothes, glassware and furniture had all been left behind. What precipitated the departure? The fire? An impulsive decision to flee this place and its harshness?

Later, talking with Vincent Gianella, a retired University of Nevada geologist who has spent many years exploring the Black Rock Desert, I collected a few more pieces of the puzzle. "I remember seeing a light from that cabin—it was sometime before 1940," he recalled. "You could see it from fifteen miles off. But when I was at the spring in 1940 there was nobody there. The house had two or three rooms. There was no fireplace and it wasn't painted. There was a stove and a bunk but not much else in the way of furniture. I think it was occupied sporadically by a rancher and his family. They had kerosene lamps, no generator. There was a fenced horse corral and a fenced garden. He must have run cattle or sheep out there, grazing them up in the hills. I went back there in 1959 but it had burned down by then."

The anonymous settler had undoubtedly perceived what his human predecessors at Black Rock Spring had learned to their sorrow—the place was too strong for them. "This place did not dance to any tune that men called," Stewart wrote. The sight of the Black Rock Desert had unnerved John Frémont, who confessed that "the appearance of the country was so forbidding that I was afraid to enter it." The pioneers and miners who followed him were not always so prudent—they came through the desert by the thousands.

Prospectors were lured to Black Rock country by wispy tales drifting in the dust of the pioneers. The children in one emigrant party, according to folklore, tossed pebbles from a canyon wall into a blue bucket dangling at the side of a wagon. When they reached California the emigrants discovered that the pebbles were gold, but hot-eyed prospectors could never find the same canyon. Forty-niner James Hardin plucked some soft stones from a ravine near Black Rock Spring and melted them into bullets. Years later, after Hardin had moved to California, one of the bullets fell into the hands of an assayer and proved to be an amalgam of silver and lead. Scores of miners and investors surged into the Black Rock Range. They built three ore mills and even raised a town called Hardin City, 10 miles north of Black Rock, but the ore proved worthless and the mines closed within two years.

The Black Rock region, with its dry mountains bordered by hundreds of narrow canyons, ravines and gullies, was one of the last arenas of confrontation between Indians and whites. Most Great Basin tribes were peaceful, but in 1865 and 1866 white settlers and cavalry fought a series of battles in northwestern Nevada with Paiute, Bannock and Shoshone. One band of Paiute was led by a warrior named Black Rock Tom, who rode a beautiful white horse and terrorized cavalry and ranchers alike for almost a year. As late as 1911 a group of renegade Bannock braves murdered four white sheepmen, then eluded a posse for two weeks in the desert before they were tracked down.

I walked from the burned cabin back to my campsite. The heat of the afternoon was finally abating, and I felt an urge to *will* the sun below the mountains. I washed off the dirt and ashes with a bucket of hot spring water, and enjoyed the pink glow of the encircling sunset. I cooked my final dinner in Black Rock and watched the mountains turn to sharp-edged silhouettes in the deep blue twilight. The soft light painted a bold, dark border around every bulrush stem. The sheepherder's wagon was outlined even more sharply. It looked at once sturdy and plaintive, an everlasting monument to human audacity in this somber country. I tried to call up a coyote with a four-inch-long whistle-like "varmint caller," which I had acquired while writing a story on the animal for LIFE, but there were no takers. I lay by the campfire for a long time, watching the night fill with light and congratulating myself for my good sense in being there. At that moment it seemed to me that I had perfect freedom and perfect peace.

Just before dawn on the day that Alvin was to pick me up I was awakened by a tremendous whooshing sound that seemed to be about five feet away. I looked blearily out of my tent in time to see a nighthawk accelerate above the hummocks. I got up soon afterward and took a last hike on the cindered sides of the rock.

I saw Alvin's Jeep perhaps five miles out on the desert, a red ant inching inexorably toward me, and stifled an impulse to climb higher up the rock and hide behind a boulder. I watched him pull up to my campsite and glance around. Finally, feeling like a reluctant captive of civilization, I climbed down and joined him at the tent.

"I got here a bit early," he said. "I thought you'd be glad to see me."

The Many Faces of a Marsh

PHOTOGRAPHS BY DAN McCOY

On the northwestern edge of sagebrush country lies an immense oasis of meadowlands, lakes and ponds. Shaped like a lopsided T whose long axis extends across 41 miles, this sprawling enclave in southeastern Oregon forms the heart of Malheur National Wildlife Refuge; covering some 180,000 acres, it is the largest wetland refuge in the Great Basin.

The refuge lies in the bowl of Harney Basin, a 600-square-mile plateau originally created when layers of lava spilled out over the land from deep cracks in the earth's surface. Ten thousand years ago, after the last ice age, glacial melt filled the basin with an enormous lake. More recently, warmer and drier conditions lowered the water level, leaving a soggy plain and three residual lakes—Malheur (right), Harney (page 126) and the much smaller Mud Lake lying between them. Although old benchmarks on the surrounding mountains indicate a former water depth of as much as 50 feet, the present lakes are mere remnants. Malheur Lake, for instance, which covers an expanse 12 by 20 miles at its greatest extent, is rarely deeper than six feet. Indeed, it is so shallow that it can hardly be called a lake at all; wildlife specialists refer to Malheur as one of the largest inland marshes in the United States.

Like all marshlands, Malheur with its sister lakes sustains a rich array of life forms. By biological standards, their productivity—or output of plant and animal life measured in pounds per acre per day—is twice as high as that of the most fecund forest. In the shallows, cattails, bulrushes and other reedy plants take root. Anchored loosely in the muddy bottoms, they crowd the surface of the water like a thick carpet and provide shelter, protection and nourishment for a large and varied animal population—mammals such as deer and rabbits, water birds like coots, herons and ibises.

Beneath the surface of the water thrives another intricate community, invisible to the casual eye. It includes pondweed, which provides a major diet item for migrating ducks; insects whose names describe their means of locomotion: whirligigs, backswimmers and water striders; and scores of species of worms and microscopic algae. On the oozy bottom, the debris of dead animals and rotting plants restores nutrients to the marsh, stimulating new growth, replenishing it and keeping its plant and animal community in balance.

The blue water of Malheur Lake captures and distorts the reflection of hardstem bulrush. This abundant grass is favored for nesting and food by waterfowl, wading birds and muskrats.

Welcome Water from the Mountains

Water is the lifeblood of the Malheur marshes. But the area's annual rainfall of nine inches hardly suffices: the moisture that regenerates the marshes every spring originates as snow in nearby mountains.

To the south looms Steens Mountain *(left)*. Down its western slope flow 14 streams that join to form the Donner und Blitzen River *(right)*, one of the marshes' principal feeders. The river was given its name—German for thunder and lightning—by a United States cavalryman who crossed it during a storm. Called the Blitzen, it winds for 35 miles to Malheur Lake. There it joins the Silvies River, which rushes from the Blue Mountains 100 miles north.

The rivers' flow varies with snowfall, which can be as little as a few inches or more than 10 feet. And the effect of this variation on the lake is dramatic: Malheur's waters covered only 500 acres in 1931 and 67,000 acres 21 years later. But Malheur benefits from these conditions. Just as a field must lie fallow to regenerate its essential elements, so the periodic drying up of a marsh allows oxygen to revitalize the bottom soil.

Thin streams trickle down Steens Mountain to join with the Blitzen River. Snow patches usually remain on the mountain throughout the summer.

A deep, sinuous gash cut into lava rock, the Blitzen River winds through dry terrain dotted with junipers, aspen and willows—as well as sagebrush.

Hardstem bulrush grows around the edges of a watery patch in Cottonwood Pond, a 185-acre combination of reedy vegetation and open water in the Blitzen Valley. Many such marshes punctuate the river's channel as it makes its way—dividing then merging —toward Malheur Lake to the north.

Mouths agape and wings flapping, three baby great-blue herons clamor for their next meal.

An American coot and her two chicks swim amid the rushes, leaving behind gentle wakes.

Two gaudy yellow-crowned blackbirds perch upon a blade of cattail grass.

Four eggs laid by a white-faced ibis are almost hidden in a tangle of bulrush. The ibis is protected at Malheur, and a small colony of this threatened species has gradually been increasing.

A jack rabbit hides amid the grasses. A ground squirrel stretches up alertly.

A female mule deer hovers protectively alongside her week-old spotted fawn.

Wild roses bloom beside a flooded field in the Blitzen Valley. The ripe hips, exposed as flowers die, are eaten by quails and pheasants.

Malheur's Partner —Harney Lake

In 1881, the story goes, a cattleman standing on the sandy reef between Malheur and Harney lakes idly kicked the ground with his boot and water began to flow through the scuff mark. It has been doing so ever since, say the natives. In all probability, it has been doing so for many thousands of years, for Harney Lake is an overflow basin for Malheur. Indeed, Harney gets most of its water this way, the only other sources being two diminutive creeks that carry snowmelt from the mountains.

As a consequence of this limited inflow, Harney is much smaller than Malheur Lake. During dry spells it almost disappears. But about three or four years in 10 Harney covers a full 30,000 acres. In wet years, Malheur Lake spills over into Harney, flushing out quantities of minerals and thus keeping its own waters fresh and sweet. Harney has no outlet whatever and evaporation has so intensified the alkalis and salts in its waters that the lake is nearly devoid of vegetation. But even this water supports certain shrimp and insects that nourish the many water birds that visit the refuge.

A sandbar surfaces in the middle of Harney Lake in a dry year. On its crest, alkali-resistant greasewood, tumbleweed and salt grass take hold.

Along the side of Harney Lake, the surfaces of wind-blown sand dunes ripple in perfect symmetry, disturbed only by the tracks of a small rodent.

In a dust storm at Harney Lake, high winds scoop up the fine alkali powder that has formed on the bottom of the lake. The purplish streaks in the foreground are damp areas in the mud flat. The blue stripe across the center is a mirage—a common sight at Malheur, where the afternoon sun's rays are refracted in heat waves so as to create a reflection of the blue sky that shimmers along the ground.

Then something happene
thing lifted their heads in p
silent command had been
that, their heads canted to
trusion. With a sudden bu
of dust and surging hoofs
side of the canyon toward
ing, crushing the foliage i
fear. Dust rolled up from t
hung behind them where
They reached the ridge in
through binoculars, frozen
the sound of their hoofs d
churning silhouettes agair
were gone, the heavily set

These wild horses, like
idents from *Homo sapien*
of survival. Each survivo
ferently. To pull throug
characteristics, trump car

With wild horses, perh
ganization, which has do
domination of his harem
far beyond keeping the r
watch for all danger, be i
Moreover the dominant
his harem until he dies o

Besides this very stabl
es have a generous allo
capacity to take hardsh
winter-kill (i.e., die of sta

"People can't grasp th
chewed up, its scraggly
Steve Pellegrini. "But th
horse that has to be toug

Another quality of wi
rough-cut rancher a littl
will sometimes resist ca
hibitively high fences, r
Then, just as suddenly, i

5.

Millions of suns f
come, by the slow pr
to desert e:

We had ridden about t
near Smoke Creek Des
We paused a few minut
then began a slow clir
named Jimmy Williams
on," he whispered. "If
from the top."

We rode on in cool m
hens fluttering indigna
liams signaled us to di
below the canyon rim.
the crest, peered over
down there," he whis;
the way up here and th

Photographer Bill E
Williams' side and loo
row grass-flecked can
the morning sun.

The scene is fixed in
color of the Western la
omino. They stood ab
five colts and a stallior

The controversial aspect of this gentle animal is that he looms as a major threat to the bighorn sheep, the quail, certain lizards and small mammals and even a few plant species. The wild burro's voracious appetite for both plants and water exerts enormous pressure on all other wildlife sharing its range.

Bighorn lovers are the most vociferous of the wild burro's enemies. They maintain that the bighorn's natural instinct, contrary to popular belief, is to roam widely rather than remain isolated on the mountain crags where it has been forced to retreat in recent times. The bighorn is far more particular about its food than the wild burro, sharing the tendency of many hoofed animals to seek quality as well as quantity. Therefore, if the burro has eaten its way through vegetation favored by the bighorn, the sheep is in trouble. To bolster their position the bighorn's defenders cite the animal's decline in population—although a good part of that decline was due to man and his gun, despite increased and stringent hunting laws. The latest figures show between 3,000 and 3,500 desert bighorn in sagebrush country, mostly in the mountains of southern Nevada and in the vicinity of Death Valley.

The wild-burro aficionado just as stoutly maintains that the animal is an important part of the American heritage and must be preserved. Patricia Moehlman, a zoologist who made an 18-month study of Death Valley's wild burros and musters a strong case for them, wrote of her belief in the right of the wild burro to exist: "We might remember that Equus, the genus to which all the asses, horses and zebras belong, originally evolved on this continent."

The National Park Service, charged with finding a solution to the problem as it exists in Death Valley, is now trying to devise ways to preserve both the wild burro and the bighorn. If the Park Service determines that the burros are taking too big a toll on their environment, it may decide to manage them within fenced areas or to control the population by judicious culling. This controversy, not as well defined as the one between wild-horse fancier and rancher—and certainly much less publicized—may be even more difficult to resolve.

No arguments flare in sagebrush country over another notable survivor, the pronghorn. Everyone agrees it must be protected. Historically, the pronghorn has survived because of its remarkable eyesight and speed. A pronghorn gives the impression of always seeing before it is seen. If a herd of pronghorn permits you to approach, as happened to me on one glorious occasion in that small area of southeastern Oregon

Pronghorn antelope raise a cloud of dust as they dash for safety, their distinctive rumps gleaming in the sunlight. Before a frightened pronghorn bolts, the animal dances a few nervous steps in a circle while the white, three-inch-long hairs lying along its rump rise up to become clearly visible, a danger signal that will alert keen-eyed companions up to a mile away.

Three wild burros, descendants of miners' pack animals, pause during a meal of blackbrush leaves in Wild Rose Canyon.

into which the Great Basin juts, it is probably because their curiosity has temporarily overcome their apprehension.

Driving along a road near Fort Rock, I rounded a curve and discovered a large winter herd of between 100 and 150 pronghorn grazing placidly in a rancher's pasture. I stopped my car and stared. They were light tan, with white chests and rumps and black hoofs. I was surprised at their size, only about three feet high at the shoulders. There was something delicate, even dainty, about their bearing and movement. Their horns curved out from their forehead and then inward, like a heart with a link missing at the top.

The pronghorn stared back at me, and began to mill nervously, still keeping their eyes on me. Then, with astonishing speed they formed themselves into a single-file column extending perhaps 100 yards. It appeared to be organized, though the means of organization was a mystery. I saw no signal and looked in vain for a pronghorn parade marshal, though in a herd that large there must have been several. After a few seconds an orderly exodus began. They departed one at a time, those waiting their turn glaring at me, the intruder who had disrupted their meal. Within three minutes the entire herd had left the pasture and I could see them loping easily across the sagebrush.

The pronghorn, indigenous to North America and now concentrated on the Western plains, is often incorrectly called the pronghorn antelope. It is a separate species, only remotely related to the genus Bovidae, which includes the true antelope of Asia and Africa. Two characteristics in particular differentiate it from the antelope: the yearly shedding of its horn sheath and its branched—or pronged—horns.

The swiftest hoofed animal in North America, the pronghorn seems to enjoy speed for its own sake. Three scientists driving across an Oregon playa once watched in fascination as a pronghorn buck kept pace with them at 50 and then 55 miles per hour. When their speed reached 60 miles per hour the buck suddenly shifted into still higher gear and cut in front of the car. Having proved whatever it was he wanted to prove, the buck cruised to a stop and stared at them from a nearby knoll.

It is an astonishing fact that pronghorn kids can keep up with their mothers when they are only a month old. In their first few helpless days, though, before they reach that degree of independence, their grayish-brown color helps protect them from coyotes, bobcats and cougars. The kids, almost always twins, benefit even more from a deliberately deceptive nonchalance on the part of their mother. In order not to attract a predator's attention to her defenseless young, the mother normally forages 400 or 500 yards, even half a mile, away from her hidden offspring. She can safely do this because of her incredible speed and eyesight. The pronghorn's large eyes (as big as a horse's) protrude from its skull, giving it an angle of vision of some 200°. And its distance vision is truly phenomenal. As long as the terrain is relatively flat and the vegetation low, the mother can easily spot the slightest suspicious object or movement at a mile or more, and if true danger arises can dash to the kid's aid.

She continues her attitude of feigned nonchalance even when feeding them. "A doe will wander over to where a kid is lying as if it wasn't there," says Pete Carter, manager of the 34,000-acre Sheldon National Antelope Refuge in northwestern Nevada. "The kid will nurse for 30 seconds and then the doe will move off, just as casual as can be. If you didn't know what was happening you wouldn't see it." The milk, it seems, is so nutritious that four or five brief feedings a day are all the young need: two or three weeks later, infancy over, they are big and strong enough to begin grazing.

Pete went on to tell me that the pronghorn has yet another intriguing characteristic that aids survival: its coat serves as air conditioner, insulator and signaling device. The strands of hair contain large air cells that protect the animal from extremes of both heat and cold. In winter the hair lies flat and warm in overlapping layers, while in summer it can stand erect, permitting air to circulate next to the skin.

Like a wild stallion, a pronghorn buck assembles and keeps a harem together during the breeding season. Acquisition of does may involve two bucks sparring for dominance, but such contests are rarely fatal. Carter told me that he once found two bucks locked together, the prongs of one hooked under the jaw of the other: one was dead, the other alive, and Pete twisted the terrified survivor free. But unlike horses the pronghorn males drift away from the does after mating, though they remain members of the same large winter herd. Pronghorn society is, in other ways, less rigidly structured than that of the wild horse: even the bigger herds are disjointed, made up of flexible smaller groups. In winter it is not unusual to see a mature doe leading a herd while a big buck brings up the rear. In the spring and summer the pronghorn may form themselves into doe herds, nursery herds (with at least one adult doe in attendance) and bachelor herds.

The pronghorn's most serious weakness is curiosity; they are drawn to any unusual activity in their territory. "We'll take a bulldozer out on

A male sage grouse fans out his tail feathers and prepares for a mating dance. Parading across an open area that he and scores of other males have selected as a dancing ground, he puffs out the long, pale sacks on each side of his chest and then expels air in two quick popping sounds—his mating call. The one or two males with the most impressive displays mate with nearly 75 per cent of the females.

their range to dig a water hole," says Carter, "and they'll gather on a hillside and watch it the way people watch construction work." Unfortunately a hunter can exploit this curiosity by flagging a buck with an attention-grabbing piece of cloth.

In the early 1800s the pronghorn numbered as many as 30 million, a figure extrapolated from explorers' and pioneers' journals, but they declined rapidly as settlers killed them for meat and as domestic cattle and sheep usurped their range. In more recent years, sharply enforced hunting limits have helped them to endure, and their population has been relatively stable for the last 10 years. Refuges like Sheldon, which was established in 1931, have been essential in achieving that stability. "There are about 5,300 pronghorn in the basin now," says federal wildlife biologist James Yoakum, "and that's just about what the range can support. They're holding their own."

A far more homely sagebrush-country resident, doing rather better than holding its own, is the kangaroo rat. The funny-looking little creature has a head as long as its body, a tail as long as both and, like its namesake, muscular, oversized hind legs. Yet the kangaroo rat is a superior survivor, even better adapted to its environment than the magnificent wild horse, the stolid wild burro and the fleet pronghorn.

There are two major reasons for the rodent's success. It is almost wholly free from the need for water and completely nocturnal. The kidneys of the kangaroo rat require very little water, and the animals have no sweat glands. They synthesize the small amount of water they need from the starch of seeds and plants they eat, and produce more through the oxidation of fats in their bodies. Their nocturnal habits keep them off the surface of the desert during the heat of the day. Thus, their adaptation to an arid country is textbook perfect.

A wholly North American creature, the kangaroo rat measures 12 to 14 inches long from its whiskered nose to the tufted tip of its skinny tail. The tail serves as a balancing mechanism when the animal rests on its haunches, and as a kind of rudder when it makes the spring-footed leaps that occasioned its name. Although the rats' customary form of locomotion is a scoot reminiscent of a mechanical toy with invisible wheels, their long hind feet can propel them in bounds covering as much as a yard when they are alarmed. The cause for this alarm, besides coyotes, might be rattlesnakes, kit foxes or owls.

When fighting or playing, kangaroo rats often leap straight up into the air, sometimes one over the other. At play they will touch noses, then suddenly spring up and back in a high leap. On other occasions they may bounce a foot or two into the air for no discernible reason other than sheer exhilaration.

The living quarters of a kangaroo rat are unmistakable; I saw them frequently in the low deserts of the southern basin. In making them, the animals first clear the vegetation from an area perhaps 20 feet in diameter to gain an unobstructed view around the burrow entrances. Then they construct a network of tunnels, chambers and passageways, sometimes as deep as four feet underground, piling the excavated dirt on top to form large mounds. Each of the several openings is large enough to accommodate a tenant that may have to enter hurriedly in the semi-upright posture it assumes when escaping a predator.

Kangaroo rats live alone except for the few weeks when young are being raised; otherwise there is no society among them. Shielded from the sun in cool, deep burrows from sunrise to sunset, they emerge to spend the night foraging for seeds, stems, buds, berries and other food that they carry in cheek pouches to shallow pits and to chambers within the burrows. (A side benefit of below-ground storage is that food, dried in the desert air, absorbs water from humidity in the burrow.) Disappearing into their bunkers at daybreak, the rats often close some entrances with dirt to discourage intruders. If you poke an entrance open the occupant often closes it again.

The kangaroo rats' distaste for illumination is so pronounced that they will remain underground on nights when the moon is particularly bright. To test the development of this behavior, California naturalist Edmund Jaeger once caught a baby kangaroo rat—which emerges from the womb the size of a walnut—and put it in a wire cage. For two weeks the infant was playful during the day, then suddenly it became completely nocturnal, thrashing and scraping the sand in its cage throughout the night. The sleepless rat watcher finally gave up and let the animal go, having observed that it had taken only a fortnight for the orphan, without a parent to imitate, to assume the natural nocturnal behavior of its species.

Another solitary night creature, and a formidable survivor, is the much misunderstood scorpion. The scorpion is feared and loathed because it is dangerous, but the danger is overrated. Though the sting can be painful, it is rarely fatal (only two species in the United States, both found in Arizona, can kill a human). The myths that have grown around this passive and most primitive of land arachnids are ancient: when surrounded by fire, it will sting itself to death (false); the female devours the male after mating (false); the young, carried on the mother's back (true), feed upon her body (false).

Scorpions are scattered mostly throughout the warmer regions of the world: in sagebrush country they live in sand dunes and on desert floors, almost always burrowing to stay out of the sun. They range in length from a half inch to eight inches; their weapons are a pair of large claws tipped by smaller pincers and a long, whiplike tail with the notorious venomous stinger at the end. They feed upon insects and spiders, grasping small victims in their claws and eating them immediately. Larger prey must be stung and paralyzed before being devoured.

Itself preyed upon by owls and raccoons, which are unaffected by its venom, the scorpion spends most of its out-of-burrow time under rocks or brush. It is completely antisocial; males and females meet only to breed. In this bizarre ceremony, the male seizes the female with his foreclaws and dances her back and forth over his extruded sperm mass until she accepts it, a ritual biologists call *promenade à deux*. The young are born living and stay with the mother only about a week.

Though the scorpion also flourishes in sagebrush country, its habitat is enormous—in fact, worldwide. One species has been found as far north as Alberta, Canada. It seems to be able to adjust to many conditions of terrain and climate, and has adapted almost as well to rain forest and jungle as to arid desert. This flexibility—and the relaxed fatalism that accompanies it—may be the key to its success. In sagebrush country a scorpion leaves its burrow at sunset and crawls casually about nearby, seeming to wait for something to happen. Since the scorpion doesn't require food and water every day, if no prey appears it simply holes up and tries its luck the next day. Its staying power is overwhelming: it has flourished for 400 million years. Perhaps the scorpion has proved itself the best adapted of all animals. I sometimes wonder if it will outlast us all.

Kingdom of the Stallion

In the desert and mountain fastnesses of the Great Basin, a gallant survivor of the Wild West still roams the land. It is the wild horse, a living symbol of the frontier virtues: independence, toughness and a readiness to fight. Though drastically reduced in numbers—some 16,000 in 1969 versus as many as two million that flourished throughout the West in the 19th Century—these enduring creatures live just as they did 100 years ago. Compact, alert and wonderfully fleet of foot, they wander in wide-ranging bands, each dominated by a stallion who competes—often with violence—for the possession of mares and collects a family unit known as a harem, ruling it as long as he has the strength to prevail.

Only four centuries ago there were no wild horses in the Americas, although the species had originally evolved here. For unknown reasons, by about 8,000 years ago all the horses in the Western Hemisphere had died out or migrated across the Bering Strait land bridge to Asia and thence into Europe.

They did not reappear until the 16th Century, when the Spanish conquistadors rode into the Americas on the spirited Andalusian horse, a magnificent mix of the hot-blooded Arabian steed and the North African Barb. Inevitably, some of their mounts escaped; others were traded to or stolen by the Indians. As the runaways multiplied, America again became home for the wild horse.

The desert blood of these horses has allowed them to thrive in sagebrush country. The scarcity of water bothers them not a bit; they can get by on shrubs, weeds and leaves. Moreover, the wild horse is inured to the most desiccating heat; its sturdy legs can take the pounding on the rough terrain; and it has even managed to adapt to the bitter winters.

The wild horse's durability is due in part to its small stature: while thoroughbreds may stand 17 hands high (about six feet measured from the base of the mane) and weigh 1,100 to 1,300 pounds, wild horses generally measure less than 15 hands and weigh only 650 to 1,100 pounds.

Some equestrian purists deride the wild horse as a scruffy runt, an inbred mongrel, but to the wilderness lover the wild horse is as inspiring today as it was in 1839 when a traveler on the Santa Fe Trail wrote, ". . . a domestic horse will ever lack that magic and indescribable charm that beams like a halo around the simple name of freedom."

Rearing in rage, two stallions engage in the fierce one-on-one combat that is at the center of their way of life. Here, the palomino (back to camera) has intruded on a water hole where the pinto and his mares were drinking. Infuriated at this breach of territory, the pinto attacks, hoofs slashing.

Snorting a danger signal, a stallion (right) wheels to defend his ground while his harem flees.

As his mares move off, an alert stallion glares down a threat—in this case the photographer.

Master of the Desert Harem

Wild-horse society is a secure bastion of absolute male supremacy. The basic social unit, the harem, consists of up to eight or more females and their offspring—called foals when very young and colts or fillies later, depending on their sex. The master of the harem is a single stallion.

From the time he comes of age at six or seven years, a male horse's primary goals are to acquire and hold a harem. The stallion keeps the band together, sternly confining it to a seasonal territory that varies with the availability of good pasturage. He constantly watches over his mares and young, herding them together whenever they straggle, his neck stretched out and weaving like the body of a snake as he nudges and nips his charges into place. He also acts as a sentinel. When he spies danger, he gives the band a signal by snorting, whistling or sharply raising his head. In response, the lead mare—usually an older horse—directs the group to safety. Before following his harem, the stallion remains to confront the danger, his position at the rear also allowing him to keep an eye on them.

The only time the mares are allowed out of his sight is in the spring, when they go off alone to foal, staying away for as little as a few days or as long as several months. Otherwise they seem content to remain with the stallion. In return for their obedience, they receive a full measure of protection and allegiance that has been crucial to the survival of their kind.

A fleet stallion guards the getaway of his band. Wild horses can gallop at speeds up to 35 mph, but only for a few minutes at a time.

A black mare, her tapering nose indicating Spanish ancestry, guards her foal. Mares usually give birth to a single foal every 18 months.

Relaxed but watchful, a harem of mares and young keep a close formation regulated by their stallion. These mares are all bays or browns, the most common colors among wild horses. For unknown reasons, some stallions seem to select only mares of a single shade, not necessarily their own.

A stallion stands guard while his harem drinks at a water hole. Horses come for water at least every other day, taking turns drinking in an established order: first mares and foals, then fillies and colts and finally the stallion. If another band arrives, it usually waits nearby to avoid a confrontation.

An older bay mare hurries two other mares and a foal away from danger over rough terrain. The stallion, typically, has remained behind

—out of sight in this photograph—to ensure his harem's safety. If a foal straggles from the pack, the stallion will chase it back in.

Two young studs playfully practice fighting, roughly bumping their flanks and bucking.

The Young Studs' Rites of Passage

When a stallion's male offspring come of age, he ejects them from his harem. Colts stay with their parents until they are about three, when they reach breeding age and begin to challenge their fathers with rough play.

Being essentially social creatures but not yet strong enough to acquire female companions, the colts, now called studs, spend several years roaming in small bands, maturing and developing the fighting skills they will need to defeat older stallions and win mares. They engage in mock combat, rearing, biting and pummeling each other with their hoofs. They may even act in tandem to raid a harem and share a captured mare, but soon each will want absolute dominion over his own harem.

When the studs are six or seven, they are ready to take on older stallions in earnest. Sometimes a threatening display is enough: if fighting ensues, it is seldom to the death; usually the weaker horse runs off.

Thus the cycle of wild-horse life goes on. Older stallions no longer able to defend and maintain a harem may spend their last years roaming alone, supplanted by the new generation. But each has had his few years of undisputed power.

While a mare and foal look on, an angry black stallion circles back into a fray begun by three young studs who had attacked him. He has already downed one, who was then roughly set upon by his fellows, and he now returns to further punish the rebels.

Two wild-horse bands gallop across the sage flats of their summer pasture on the California-Nevada border. When the first snow covers their forage, they will head for the nearby mountains to feed on the grasses that are kept exposed by high winds.

6/ The Inner Life of Death Valley

---

*It requires an exercise of strongest faith to believe that
the great Creator ever smiled upon it.*

WILLIAM MANLY/ *DEATH VALLEY IN '49*

Death Valley is at once a dramatic natural phenomenon and a powerful symbol in the American imagination. Its physical credentials are formidable—the hottest and driest spot in the United States and the lowest point in the Western Hemisphere. From one end to the other, it appears as an unyielding slice of desert that penalizes the unlucky and the unprepared; more than any other corner of sagebrush country, it epitomizes the severity and starkness of that arid realm.

And no other stretch of the entire American wilderness has a stronger grip on the popular psyche. Indeed the valley has come to represent a sort of nightmare land, a province of myth and dread. The name itself, bestowed by a member of a stranded and suffering band of fortyniners, has continually reinforced the image. So have the names of places within and around the valley's confines—Last Chance Range, Coffin Canyon, Starvation Canyon, Arsenic Spring, the Devil's Cornfield (he appears to be a major landowner), Dante's View, Hell's Gate. The Indians, too, viewed the valley with trepidation, calling it Tomesha, Ground Afire. By any name, the valley is a compelling, intriguing place—although I suspect its dark repute derives as much from overheated imaginations as from overheated rock and sand.

Death Valley lies at the outermost reaches of the Great Basin, just inside California's border with southwestern Nevada. From the surrounding mountains it does not look particularly prepossessing. Only 154 miles long, it is surprisingly narrow—no more than 20 miles at the widest point and two miles at the narrowest, a mere sliver of pearl-colored desert. The Panamint Range on its west and the Funeral, Grapevine and Black mountains to the east are so close that in the distance they appear to fuse together. The endless expanses that we associate with deserts—as in the Mojave or Sahara—are missing here.

Nor is that the only way in which Death Valley confounds expectations. Its basic construction is unlike that of most other valleys. Commonly, valleys are carved out by rivers or glaciers; this one was formed by the heavings of the earth—by the faulting and uplifting of the bordering mountains, and the consequent sinking of the area between. The geologists' term for such a sunken section of the earth's crust is a graben, German for trench or trough. In effect, Death Valley is a deep ditch—very deep. Some 500 square miles lie below sea level, reaching a nadir of 282 feet below sea level near Badwater in the south-central part of the valley. Yet only about 15 miles away towers the highest peak in the Panamint Range—11,049-foot Telescope Peak. The difference in elevation is spectacular even for the Great Basin, where alternating mountains and plains are the standard pattern.

The depth of Death Valley is what primarily accounts for its phenomenal heat. Anywhere in the world, with every 1,000-foot drop in elevation the temperature tends to rise 3½° F. The situation in Death Valley is compounded by the embracing mountain walls. These barriers box in the air that naturally becomes denser and warmer as it descends from the heights.

Other factors intensify the furnace effect. About 200 square miles of the valley floor are covered with deposits of white salt, which serve as relentless heat reflectors when the sun blazes down. The cooling influence normally exerted by vegetation and rainfall is almost nil; rainfall here is a barely existent 1.68 inches a year, and vegetation is correspondingly sparse. Death Valley does enjoy milder temperatures in winter months, but thereafter the thermometer starts soaring. By July, the average daily high is 116° F. The highest air temperature ever recorded was 134.6°, on a July day in 1913. Temperatures taken of the ground are still more fiery: they have gone as high as 190°. Even with thick-soled boots, walking the valley can be a foot-frying experience.

The heat of both ground and air tend to repel what little rain does attempt to fall—the air heat vaporizes some of the drops before they touch bottom, and the ground heat causes the remnants to evaporate instantaneously. As a result, there are very few patches of valley terrain

Winds ripple the surface of sand dunes near Tucki Mountain, on Death Valley's western edge. The dunes, some of them more than 120 feet high, consist of fine particles of granite and sandstone washed into the valley from the surrounding mountains and swept to Tucki's base by the wind.

that are not persistently bone dry. And the traveler who neglects to take along his own ample water supply does so at his peril. Even with this precaution, and after only a few hours of valley scenery, he finds himself thinking—close to hallucinating—about sparkling streams and lakes and ponds he has known in greener climes. His sense of deprivation is not quite allayed by the sight of snow lingering on the crests of the neighboring Panamint peaks as late as May.

Once in a great while, storms will loose an avalanche of snow on a mountain slope, or a cloudburst will send a flood racing down a canyon. My friend Pete Sanchez, who has roamed the valley almost daily since 1969, says: "You can see a dry canyon turn into a torrent four or five feet deep, with two-hundred-pound boulders crashing along and the water so turbid that it is white, opaque. Then, just as quickly, the place is all dry debris, as if nothing had happened. And nothing has —except that the canyon is eroded a fraction of an inch deeper."

The potential for sudden savagery, the blistering heat and the miles of parched wastes summon up a picture of Death Valley that is undeniably daunting. Yet there is also beauty in this stripped-down landscape, an elemental beauty that invites the viewer to enjoy form and color, texture and pattern for their own sakes. No lush foliage distracts the eye from the soft sweep of a dune, the bold jut of an ancient rock mass. The sand, salt and gravel of the valley floor are cleanly perceived; the wilderness traveler becomes aware of the varied attributes of these commonplace substances, their subtle gradations of gray and white and beige.

One day I walked across the base of one of the broad, gently sloping alluvial fans that rise on both sides of the valley, great aprons of gravel that billow out from the canyons. Suddenly I realized that the ground just below my feet was a shiny dark brown—an effect produced by so-called desert varnish. This is a patina of iron and manganese oxide leached out of underlying rocks and brought to the surface by water seeping up, so that over the course of years the gravel becomes coated. On other parts of the fan I saw stretches of the formation called desert pavement, similar to that I had encountered during my sojourn in Black Rock Desert. The stones were inlaid on a level surface that resembled a piece of terrazzo flooring. They fit together so neatly that they yield no dust to the winds coming out of the canyons. "It's nature's defense mechanism against excessive erosion in the desert," Pete Sanchez says.

Of all the valley's surprises, to me the most stunning is the light-and-color show that unfolds as each day progresses. I watched a sunrise at

Zabriskie Point, amid a cluster of bare siltstone hills on the valley's east side. The Panamints, looking close enough to touch, were the color of a newly minted penny. Sunlight descended the mountain wall in such an orderly progression it seemed a caretaker might be flipping on a switch at successive floors; when the light hit the valley, the surface glistened as if a stage made of mother-of-pearl had been uncovered. The light spread over the hills near me, striping their pitted faces like shop awnings. A dozen shades of brown ranging from sand to chocolate emerged from the recesses. With the sun full in the sky the darkest rocks looked moss green, and the Panamints turned lavender.

"Every peak, every face, every ledge, every declivity, every gorge, every strata, every rock, has a color of its own," a journalist named John Spears wrote after exploring Death Valley in 1892, "and there are no two breadths of color exactly alike. They vary from marble white to lava black, from the palest green to the darkest carmine, from the faintest cream to royal purple—there is every tint and every brilliant and every dull body of color, and all mingled, contrasted, and blended, all piled up in such magnificent masses as are beyond description."

Not many 19th Century Americans shared this admiration for the valley. The first pioneers to reach it—by Christmas Day in 1849—did not do so by design; they had been misled by a map that promised a shortcut through the Great Basin to California's gold country. One of the trekkers, William Manly, later wrote a book describing their harrowing stay in the valley. He recalled: "Ever in the minds of those who braved its heat and sands was the thought of a horrid Charnel house."

Eventually a few rugged types tried permanent residence in and around the valley, including the five euphonically named Lee brothers —Leander, Philander, Meander, Salamander and Alexander—who ran cattle and gained a generally unsavory reputation. Prospectors scoured the area for gold and silver and copper during the late 19th and early 20th centuries. But the only mineral to yield a consistent profit was borax found on the valley floor—and hauled away by the famous 20-mule teams, which took it to the nearest railroad, 165 miles away.

The tunnels and shafts of abandoned mines still dot the mountain canyons, and now and then a lonely grave marker has turned up in the valley's remoter reaches. One reads simply, "Val Nolan, a victim of the elements." The death of Alfred Nard in 1906 was attributed to "new boots," which caused Nard's feet to swell as he crossed the valley on a broiling summer day. He shed them, and before long his feet were so

The shaft entrance and workshed of a petered-out gold mine—abandoned since 1913—slowly decay in the dry desert air of Death Valley.

blistered that he could not continue. He lay down and never got up.

Lack of water has taken perhaps the heaviest toll in the valley. Men have been driven insane here by thirst; some died with full canteens on their belts. The prospect of running out of water terrifies travelers to this day. Pete Sanchez himself has faced the experience. Bicycling around the valley one afternoon, he found he had misjudged the amount of water he needed to carry along. "I ran short," he recalls. "I went four or five miles and began to feel nauseated. I lay down and had to force myself to get up. I just wanted to sleep. Finally I saw an avalanche track on a wash and found snow under some twigs. When I got home I drank and drank and wanted more—I had half a gallon of water and still felt thirsty."

Nevertheless, Sanchez stoutly contends that there is nothing hostile about Death Valley. "It is no more hostile than the Arctic or the top of a mountain," he says. "Land is not hostile; it is neutral. People who say it is hostile are unwilling to adjust to it."

As exemplars of adjustment, he cites the Shoshone Indians who occupied the valley in recent centuries, following the progression of ripening vegetation from the edges of the valley floor on up to the mountaintops. The Shoshone made a sort of porridge from the pods of the mesquite trees in the valley; the piñon trees in the mountains provided them with pine nuts. In all, they harvested 100 different species of edible plants, and now and then they embellished their diet by rabbit hunts. "It was an exquisite adaptation to the land," Sanchez says. "They had nothing unnecessary. They filled their needs, not their desires, and they lived in peace."

Sanchez talks with equal fervor about another injustice to Death Valley's reputation: to regard it as hostile is bad enough, but to think of it as lifeless is even worse. To its defense he rallies an assortment of statistics—more than 600 species of plants and more than 200 species of animals inhabit the valley and its bordering slopes. Their tenancy is not, to be sure, of a conspicuous kind. Such larger mammals as the bighorn sheep and the wild burro favor the mountains, with their isolated canyons and concealing crags, while the kit fox, the kangaroo rat and the antelope ground squirrel range the valley floor. Floor-dwelling animals like these are mostly nocturnal, hunting and foraging after dark to preserve their energies in the heat of day.

The plants, too, make their adjustments. Most species are to be found in the mountains, close to springs; the comparatively congenial growing conditions on the heights produce a variety of ferns and grasses, a profusion of flowers, including two kinds of orchids, and a plant more often associated with cool northern brooks—watercress. But the lower reaches of Death Valley are by no means bare of vegetation, except on the central salt flats—and even they harbor life below the surface in the form of algae. Elsewhere in the valley, scores of hardy species successfully defy the desert heat and drought and salt. The very names of some suggest toughness: pickleweed, brittlebush, iodine bush, creosote, desert holly, beavertail cactus, shad scale and—not least—sagebrush.

On a temperate morning in March, Sanchez and I set off for what he billed as a tour of the teeming life in Death Valley. "I could show you dozens of examples," he said, "but just two of my favorites will do. One is a tree and the other, believe it or not, is a fish."

We headed southeast from the village of Stovepipe Wells in the north-central part of the valley, picking our way across crunchy, meringue-like terrain. The valley has three distinct types of salt deposits and this one, Sanchez informed me, was the so-called sulfate zone. I looked in vain for creatures scurrying about, but my companion's eyes were better attuned. "Over there," he cried. "Lizard. Side-blotched." The small brown reptile appeared to be doing push-ups between two mounds of salt. "That's just one of seventeen species of lizard in the valley," Sanchez added, obviously enjoying this unanticipated demonstration of the valley's animal inhabitants.

We passed through the sulfate zone and onto the white popcorn-like surface of the chloride belt. We were descending by imperceptible stages to the bottom of the valley. The only visible plants were clumps of stumpy pickleweed, one of the most salt-tolerant of Death Valley species, and now even they were receding behind us.

The chloride surface, packed more tightly than the sulfate, was a hard white crust, broken frequently into geometric patterns. Some of the deposits of salt were round and grapefruit sized, some tiny and delicate like budding flowers. In other places the salt had formed hollow tubes, perhaps eight inches high, poking up from the surface like straws from a sea of milk. "Imagine leading an ox and wagon across this," Sanchez said, shaking his head.

We saw another lizard—this one gray, with the black-and-white rear markings that identify it as the zebra-tailed species. Next we saw a spider, industriously weaving a web between two protruding small hills of salt. "They have a nice little system going," Sanchez remarked. "There are algae in the marsh up ahead. The algae are nourished from

A full-grown Salt Creek pupfish, only two inches long, nibbles algae in a desert stream. The pupfish thrives in shallow streams and pools, where seasonal temperatures range from 40° to 100° F.—and where evaporation may increase the water's salinity to a point that would kill most fresh-water fish. In particularly dry summers, a pupfish lying on its side can flap its way for a few feet across rapidly shrinking puddles to find deeper water.

rock; gnats and flies live on the algae; beetles prey on the fly larvae; the spiders snare flies and beetles."

"Did you say marsh up ahead?" I asked. "I did," Sanchez said. "You know," he added, smiling, "not every inch of Death Valley is bone dry. That's just another one of the myths about the place." It seems there are a number of pools around the valley's rim, fed by underground springs; the water constantly seeps out, and in enough quantity to off-set the high rate of evaporation once it reaches the valley floor.

We began to encounter patches of mud among the salt crystals, then shallow puddles of salty water. Sanchez stepped around them, press-ing on ahead. "This is Cottonball Marsh," he called behind him. "One of the homes of the fish I wanted you to see." The marsh is named for the white puffs of salt around the pools.

Suddenly Sanchez stopped at a pool of dark brown-green water, per-haps three feet deep and six feet across, with dozens of tiny fish in it, the biggest no more than two inches long. They swarmed around the pool's crusty rim, darting out of sight when we came too near.

"Pupfish," Sanchez said. "Cottonball Marsh pupfish, a species all its own. The salt content of that water is probably five times as high as the ocean and yet they can take it."

Pupfish have been traced by fossil evidence to the Miocene epoch some 25 million years ago—awesome proof of their powers of survival. Though thousands die each summer when isolated by drying marshes and creeks, enough pools remain for the species to continue to flourish.

We knelt on the salt pan to watch the hectic activity in the pool —spawning, as it happened. The males were identifiable by their ir-idescent blue markings, the females by a lighter color. A male would stake out a territory perhaps nine inches in diameter and patrol it. If an-other male swam into the area the confrontation was immediate: the in-truder either swam away or was routed after a second's scuffle. Any female who appeared, however, was fair game. Every so often one lin-gered long enough for the male to induce her to spawn.

At intervals the male would swim to the bottom of the pool and nip at it, picking up bits of material, then spitting them out; at other times he would dig a tiny trench with his body. Fertilization is achieved when the male and female couple in an S-shaped position. The female drops her egg onto the bottom and the male releases sperm. The female then swims off. The male remains in his territory to repeat the performance with other females. The eggs hatch in about two weeks.

We violated pupfish privacy for an hour or so before moving on to our second destination. We retraced our steps partway back to Stovepipe Wells, then veered north. After a while the crunchy salt underfoot gave way to smooth sand. Clumps of arrowweed and shad scale, plants that cannot thrive too close to the salt flats, began to appear. Ravens, invariably in pairs, cruised low over our heads and croaked—inquisitively, I thought.

In the relative mildness of March, the sand beneath our boots felt merely warm, rather than burning hot. Occasionally we blundered onto the roof of a ground squirrel's underground apartment and plunged a foot deep, only then discovering a half-dozen secret entrances the occupant had dug in the sand.

Finally we came in sight of a grove of trees ranging from five to 20 feet tall, widely spaced around the dunes. Each had developed a veritable thicket of spreading branches, long green leaves and tiny yellow flowers. "Mesquite," Sanchez announced. "My second major example of the rich, full life of Death Valley." He looked at the trees with a doting expression. "If all the plants in the valley were ranked in order of importance on a scale of a hundred points," he said, "the mesquite would get a hundred and the runner-up less than ten."

The mesquite's role as life-giver and lifesaver is unique among desert plants. The Shoshone who nourished themselves on the beans in its pods were not the only human beneficiaries; prospectors used the mesquite's wood as fuel for their campfires, and its shade as a respite from the sun. Though humans no longer depend on the tree, for the animal population it remains a generous provider of food and housing. Wild burros browse on its leaves, kit foxes and rabbits and coyotes relish its pods, insects thrive on the nectar of its sweet-smelling blossoms. Kangaroo rats, pack rats, several species of wild mice, ground squirrels and the sidewinder—a member of the rattlesnake clan—make their homes in the sand mounds that accumulate around the tree's base. The mesquite itself manages to thrive in its arid environment primarily because of a remarkable system of roots, some reaching as far as 100 feet below the surface to tap the water table.

Prowling the mesquite grove, Sanchez and I found a dozen signs of occupation, human and animal. Old bottles and a makeshift well—a barrel sunk into the sand—indicated a prospector's campsite. A pack rat's assemblage of miscellaneous goods—pieces of bone, seeds, twigs—was piled beneath a low branch. Coyote scat was evidence of a visiting predator—just one of the species that turn up to pounce on the smaller creatures. Phoebes and yellow-headed verdins darted through the mesquite branches, picking off a variety of insects.

Each mesquite appeared to be a kind of village. Most of its inhabitants, to be sure, were out of sight at the moment, awaiting nightfall to emerge. But a network of tracks was clearly visible on the smooth sand. There were lizard tracks made in the shape of narrow gullies; beetle tracks, like tiny punchboards of circular dots; field-mouse tracks, delicate, petal shaped, all four footprints bunched together; kit-fox tracks, identifiable by the two front pads, an inch or two apart. In addition there were the prints of rabbits, ravens and coyotes; all had apparently had some recent business at that particular mesquite.

One track was a puzzle—a curved, lazy loop on the sand about a foot long. There was never more than one in one place, so we concluded that it wasn't the mark of a sidewinder. Though sidewinders make that sort of imprint as they shimmy along, their tracks always occur in a parallel sequence. Then what was it? The long tail of a kangaroo rat, possibly, but if so where were the footprints? It couldn't be a lizard; the track was too short to qualify as a long slither. "I don't know," Sanchez confessed. "Call it another mystery of the desert."

He stared between the trees at the valley beyond, pure pleasure written on his face. "Desolation!" he snorted. "Most people say, 'Desolation, let me out.' I say, 'Desolation, isn't it grand?' "

On an impulse I stretched out on the sand and watched a black carpenter ant struggle with the carcass of an equal-sized orange ant. With my face pressed to the desert floor, it occurred to me that from ground level a mesquite seems to scrape the sky like a redwood. Death Valley may be a desert to me, but to a carpenter ant it's a forest.

As I lay there, I suddenly thought of Mark Twain, who had viewed the life of the desert from a similar vantage point. Lying beneath a sagebrush, Twain had watched armies of insects parading around their own "monarch of the forest," and had gained an insight into the desert's true dimensions. More than a century separated Twain's adventure and mine, and much of the world had changed. But it seemed to me that the essence of sagebrush country had come through unscathed.

The Devil's Landscape

PHOTOGRAPHS BY WOLF VON DEM BUSSCHE

To most people the name conjures up a flat, forbidding place, as dull as it has been dangerous. But, as photographer Wolf von dem Bussche discovered, Death Valley is by no means all flat and nowhere dull—though it is indeed forbidding and can be ferociously hot.

When von dem Bussche arrived in the second week of May, the thermometer on a shaded porch of a general store registered 110° F. at 10 o'clock in the morning. By midday the temperature was 135° in the glare of the sun; the ground had been superheated to 180°. Even at sunset, the walled valley remained a furnace. Thus, when making his photographic forays, von dem Bussche was confined to the hours between four and seven in the morning, when the temperature was in the 90s.

At that time of day he found Death Valley yielding a kaleidoscope of colors, from the jet-black volcanic cinders of Ubehebe Crater to the golden, layered siltstone of Manly Beacon. Instead of flatness, heights loomed on every side: the 5,000-foot Black Mountains up to the 11,049 summit of Telescope Peak in the Panamint Mountains. Instead of monotony, the land revealed illusions and surprises. Seen from the mile-high Dante's View (right), the salt flats below stretched off as seemingly smooth as the surface of a misty lake. But close up, at the Devil's Golf Course, the salt surface rose and fell in a crazy jumble of mud-streaked spires two feet high. And in a supposedly barren sector of the valley that lies about 200 feet below sea level, von dem Bussche even found a creek teeming with tiny pupfish and banked with salt grass.

As the sun began to rise, it transformed the shapes of sand dunes near Tucki Mountain, changing one dark mound to an orange pyramid. Meanwhile the wind was furrowing the sand, and a gust breached the curve of a crest in a trough called a blowout. In the hollows between dunes lay cracked, baked sediments. Here and there, the roots of half-buried creosote bushes and mesquite trees reached down into the parched earth, seeking water.

In this almost surrealistic scenery, von dem Bussche noticed that his normal sense of time vanished. Cramped minutes and hours gave way to a feeling of the flow of eons. His fears, too, began to fade. "Somewhat incredulously," he says, "I realized that the beauty far surpassed the terrors of this desert."

SALT FLATS SEEN FROM THE ROCKY PRECIPICE OF DANTE'S VIEW

CRACKED SEDIMENTS AGAINST A BACKDROP OF WIND-RIPPLED SAND

MORNING SUN ON A DISTANT DUNE

THE SILTSTONE SPIRE OF MANLY BEACON

HALF-DEAD MESQUITE ATOP A DUNE

CRUSTED SILT AND A CREOSOTE BUSH

SALT CREEK AT DAYBREAK

DESERT HOLLY AND SALTBUSH NEAR UBEHEBE CRATER

SAND DUNE BREACHED BY A BLOWOUT

PINNACLES OF SALT AT THE DEVIL'S GOLF COURSE

Bibliography

*Also available in paperback.
†Available only in paperback.

Bartlett, Richard A., *Great Surveys of the American West*. University of Oklahoma Press, 1966.

†Belden, L. Burr, *Goodbye, Death Valley!* Inland Printing, 1969.

Bissell, Harold J., *Bonneville—An Ice-age Lake*. Department of Geology, Brigham Young University, 1968.

†Clark, William D., and David Muench, *Death Valley—The Story behind the Scenery*. KC Publications, Las Vegas, Nevada, 1973.

Combs, Barry B., *Westward to Promontory*. American West Publishing Company, 1969.

*Corle, Edwin, *Death Valley and the Creek Called Furnace*. Ward Ritchie Press, 1962.

*DeVoto, Bernard, *The Year of Decision: 1846*. Little, Brown and Company, 1943.

Dobie, J. Frank, *The Mustangs*. Little, Brown and Company, 1952.

Dunlop, Richard, *Great Trails of the West*. Abingdon Press, 1971.

Elliott, Russell R., *History of Nevada*. University of Nebraska Press, 1973.

Federal Writers' Project, *Nevada: A Guide to the Silver State*. Binfords & Mort, 1957.

Federal Writers' Project, *Utah: A Guide to the State*. Hastings House, 1954.

Frémont, John Charles, *Report of the Exploring Expedition to the Rocky Mountains*. University Microfilms, 1966.

Gilbert, Edmund W., *The Exploration of Western America, 1800-1850*. Cooper Square Publishers, 1966.

*Greever, William S., *Bonanza West: The Story of the Western Mining Rushes 1848-1900*. University of Oklahoma Press, 1963.

Horan, James D., *Timothy O'Sullivan: America's Forgotten Photographer*. Doubleday & Company, 1966.

Hunt, Charles B., *Physiography of the United States*. W. H. Freeman and Company, 1967.

Jackman, E. R., and John Scharff, *Steens Mountain*. The Caxton Printers, 1968.

*Jaeger, Edmund C., *Desert Wildlife*. Stanford University Press, 1961.

Jaeger, Edmund C., *A Naturalist's Death Valley*, rev. ed. Inland Printing, 1971.

*Jaeger, Edmund C., *The North American Deserts*. Stanford University Press, 1957.

Kirk, Ruth, *Desert: The American Southwest*. Houghton Mifflin Company, 1973.

†Kirk, Ruth, *Exploring Death Valley*. Stanford University Press, 1973.

†Klamath County Historical Society, Oregon, *The Applegate Trail*. 1971.

Larson, Peggy, *Deserts of America*. Prentice-Hall, 1970.

Manly, William L., *Death Valley in '49*. The Pacific Tree and Vine Company, San Jose, California, 1894.

†Miller, David E., *Great Salt Lake Past and Present*. Utah History Atlas, 1969.

*Morgan, Dale L., *The Great Salt Lake*. The Bobbs-Merrill Company, 1947.

Niering, William A., *The Life of the Marsh*. McGraw-Hill Book Company, 1966.

Putnam, George P., *Death Valley and Its Country*. Duell, Sloan and Pearce, 1946.

Rickett, Harold William, *Wildflowers of the United States: Volume 4: The Southwestern States*. The New York Botanical Garden, McGraw-Hill Book Company, 1970.

*Ryden, Hope, *America's Last Wild Horses*. E. P. Dutton & Company, 1970.

Ryden, Hope, *Mustangs: A Return to the Wild*. The Viking Press, 1972.

Spears, John R., *Illustrated Sketches of Death Valley*. Rand, McNally & Company, 1892.

*Stewart, George R., *The California Trail*. McGraw-Hill Book Company, 1962.

Stewart, George R., *Sheep Rock*. Random House, 1951.

†Stokes, William Lee, ed., *The Great Salt Lake*. Utah Geological Society, 1966.

Thornbury, William D., *Regional Geomorphology of the United States*. John Wiley & Sons, 1965.

*Twain, Mark, *Roughing It*. New American Library, 1962.

†Wheeler, Sessions S., *The Nevada Desert*. The Caxton Printers, 1971.

Bulletins and Pamphlets

Duebbert, Harold F., *The Ecology of Malheur Lake and Management Implications*. Malheur National Wildlife Refuge Leaflet No. 412, Nov. 1969.

Hunt, Charles B., T. W. Robinson, Walter A. Bowles and A. L. Washburn, *Hydrologic Basin, Death Valley, California*. Geological Survey Professional Paper 494-B, U.S. Government Printing Office, 1966.

Lewis, Mont E., *Flora and Major Plant Communities of the Ruby-East Humboldt Mountains*. Humboldt National Forest, U.S. Forest Service, 1971.

Russell, Israel Cook, *Geological History of Lake Lahontan*. U.S. Government Printing Office, 1885.

Woodman, Ruth C., *The Story of Pacific Coast Borax Co.* Ward Ritchie Press, 1951.

Acknowledgments

The author and editors of this book are particularly indebted to Alvin McLane, Reno, Nevada. They also wish to thank the following. In California: Frank Ackerman, Death Valley National Monument, Death Valley; Clyde E. Brewer, Bureau of Land Management, Susanville; Peter G. Sanchez, Death Valley National Monument, Death Valley. In Nevada: A. Clair Baldwin, U.S. Forest Service, Toiyabe National Forest, Austin; Allen Bruner, Division of Renewable Natural Resources, College of Agriculture, University of Nevada, Reno; James E. Deacon, Professor of Biology, University of Nevada, Las Vegas; Vincent P. Gianella, Professor Emeritus of Geology, University of Nevada, Reno; Carol Gunn, U.S. Forest Service, Toiyabe National Forest, Austin; E. W. Harris, Professor Emeritus of Mechanical Engineering, University of Nevada, Reno; John S. Healy, U.S. Forest Service, Toiyabe National Forest, Austin; Peter J. Herlan, Curator of Biology, Nevada State Museum, Carson City; L. James Higgins Jr., Curator of Manuscripts, Nevada Historical Society, Reno; John Houghton, Assistant Professor of Geography, University of Nevada, Reno; Darwin R. Jensen, U.S. Forest Service, Humboldt National Forest, Lamoille; Albert Neu, Soil Conservation Service, U.S. Department of Agriculture, Austin; Nevada Department of Fish and Game, Elko; Alan A. Partridge, Assistant District Ranger, Humboldt National Forest, Ely; John H. Schilling, Director of Nevada Bureau of Mines and Geology, University of Nevada, Reno; Thomas J. Trelease, Chief of Fisheries, Nevada Department of Fish and Game, Reno; Paul T. Tueller, Professor of Renewable Natural Resources, College of Agriculture, University of Nevada, Reno; Frits W. Went, Professor of Botany, University of Nevada, Reno; John T. Wilcox, District Ranger, Humboldt National Forest, Ely. In New York: Willis J. Gertsch, Curator Emeritus, The American Museum of Natural History, New York City; Ronald Hoham, Professor of Biology, Colgate University, Hamilton; Sidney S. Horenstein, Department of Invertebrate Paleontology, The American Museum of Natural History, New York City. In Oregon: Joseph Mazzoni, Refuge Manager, Malheur National Wildlife Refuge, Burns; Al Radtke, Assistant Manager, Malheur National Wildlife Refuge, Burns. In Salt Lake City, Utah: K. Haybron Adams, Assistant Supervisor, Archive Search Room, Historical Department, Church of Jesus Christ of Latter-day Saints; John D. Carlson, U.S. Bureau of Land Management; Gordon Tenny, Utah State Parks and Recreation; James Whelan, Utah Geological and Mineral Survey. And also C. W. Ferguson, Professor of Dendrochronology, Laboratory of Tree-Ring Research, University of Arizona, Tucson; Albert L. Little, U.S. Forest Service, Division of Timber Management Research, Washington, D.C.

Picture Credits

Sources for the pictures in this book are shown below. Credits for pictures from left to right are separated by semicolons; from top to bottom by dashes.

Cover—Daniel Kramer. End papers 2, 3 —Dan McCoy. End paper 4, page 1 —Richard Weymouth Brooks. 2, 3 —Barry Lopez. 4, 5—David Muench. 6, 7—Dan McCoy. 8, 9—Daniel Kramer. 10, 11—Richard Weymouth Brooks. 12, 13—Daniel Kramer. 18, 19—Maps supplied by Hunting Surveys Limited. 25 —Daniel Kramer. 29—Daniel Kramer. 33—Dick Rowan. 37 through 51—Daniel Kramer. 56, 57—Wolf von dem Bussche. 58—Bill Ratcliffe. 60, 61—Wolf von dem Bussche. 64, 65—Bill Eppridge from Time-Life Picture Agency. 66—John Hamlin. 70, 71—Courtesy of the Historical Department, The Church of Jesus Christ of Latter-day Saints. 72, 73 —Chief of Engineers in the National Archives; courtesy of the Bancroft Library, University of California, Berkeley. 74, 75—Courtesy Nevada Historical Society; courtesy Grahame Hardy. 76, 77—Courtesy Nevada Historical Society; courtesy of The Oakland Museum. 80, 81—Philip Hyde. 85—Wolf von dem Bussche. 89—David Cavagnaro. 92 through 101—David Cavagnaro. 104, 105—Dan McCoy. 108—Alvin McLane. 111—Barry Lopez. 117 through 129 —Dan McCoy. 132—Joe van Wormer. 135—George Silk from Time-Life Picture Agency. 136—Daniel Kramer. 138 —Joe van Wormer from The National Audubon Society. 143—Hope Ryden from Animals Animals. 144—Hope Ryden from Animals Animals—Bill Eppridge. 145—Hope Ryden. 146 through 149—Bill Eppridge. 150, 151—Bill Eppridge; Hope Ryden. 152, 153—Bill Eppridge. 156, 157—Wolf von dem Bussche. 160—Daniel Kramer. 162—Peter G. Sanchez. 167 through 179—Wolf von dem Bussche.

Index

*Numerals in italics indicate a
photograph or drawing of the subject
mentioned.*